PROGRAMMING BY CASE STUDIES
AN ALGOL PRIMER

INTRODUCTORY MONOGRAPHS IN MATHEMATICS

General Editor
A. J. MOAKES, M.A.

Numerical Mathematics   A. J. Moakes
    Exercises in computing with a desk calculating machine

Mathematics for Circuits   W. Chellingsworth

The Core of Mathematics   A. J. Moakes
    An introduction to 'modern' mathematics

A Boolean Algebra   A. B. Bowran
    Abstract and Concrete

Matrices and their Applications
    J. R. Branfield and A. W. Bell

PROGRAMMING BY CASE STUDIES

An Algol Primer

BY

O. B. CHEDZOY and SANDRA E. FORD

BATH UNIVERSITY OF TECHNOLOGY

MACMILLAN

© O. B. Chedzoy and Sandra E. Ford 1969

Published by
MACMILLAN AND CO LTD
Little Essex Street London WC2
and also at Bombay Calcutta and Madras
Macmillan South Africa (Publishers) Pty Ltd Johannesburg
The Macmillan Company of Australia Pty Ltd Melbourne
The Macmillan Company of Canada Ltd Toronto
St Martin's Press Inc New York
Gill and Macmillan Ltd Dublin

ISBN 978-0-333-10146-9   ISBN 978-1-349-00700-4 (eBook)
DOI 10.1007/978-1-349-00700-4

C O N T E N T S

CHAPTER		PAGE
	Preface	
1	INTRODUCTION	1
2	FUNDAMENTALS OF ALGOL	5
3	SORTING NUMBERS	14
4	THE CENTRE OF ENGLAND	20
5	EVALUATION OF PI ACCUMULATION OF INACCURACIES OF ROUND-OFF	32
6	MOVEMENTS IN A SHARE PRICE INDEX	40
7	ADDITIONAL ALGOL	47
8	SIMPLE SIMULATION: SNAKES AND LADDERS	53
9	CALIBRATION OF A DEPTH GAUGE USE OF APPROXIMATION	60
10	JOB PLANNING A PROBLEM IN OPTIMIZATION	73
11	EVALUATION OF e	84

PREFACE

In writing this book we have been aware that there are already in existence many excellent books on Algol programming. Yet amongst these, we have not found one which gives a series of case studies with programs.

In selecting the subjects under study, we have chosen those which can readily be understood and appreciated by students who are in school sixth forms. Only two of them need mathematical knowledge beyond 'O' level GCE, and even this may not be vital.

It is intended that this book can be read and studied in two ways - two Algol chapters illustrated by the examples, or as 8 case studies with two Algol reference chapters. The former method is the more conventional approach, but if Algol is recognised as a language, then the latter method has much in common with contemporary language teaching.

The case studies have been described as starting from the general problem, rather than just a mathematical statement which has to be coded. In this way, it is hoped to emphasize that the arrangement of the problem in a form which is realistic for programming is part of the task; another part lies in the writing of a program as efficient as possible at the first attempt; still another part lies in appreciating that more calculation may decrease rather than increase accuracy.

All the programs illustrated have been used in practice on an Elliott 803 B computer, and are acceptable by most (if not all) computers with Algol compilers.

In conclusion we should like to acknowledge the encouragement and help we have received from the following:

        Doreen Chedzoy
        Peter Ford
        Kate Smith
        Rosemary Westley, for typing the manuscript
and   The Computer Unit of Bath University which has provided the computer time.

Data for Chapter 6 has been taken from the Financial Times Index of Industrial Shares, with their permission.

                                        O.B. Chedzoy
                                        Sandra E. Ford

1

INTRODUCTION

1.1 Use of Algol

ALGOL is a programming language which has been designed to meet the needs of the mathematical user of a computer. As implied by its name, derived from ALGOrithmic Language, ALGOL may be used conveniently to describe the procedure to be followed for a numerical calculation. The language incorporates ordinary English words and conventional mathematical symbols which enable an Algol program to be easily comprehended. By publishing Algol programs and procedures widely throughout the computer world, it becomes possible for the work of experts to be available to anyone conversant with the language.

To make effective use of Algol it is not necessary to be familiar with computer techniques and only for certain aspects does the user require to know the specification of his chosen computer.

Algol, thus, allows a direct translation of a mathematical equation into the computation associated with it.

An equality

$a = b + c$ (a equals b plus c)

is written in Algol as a statement

$a := b + c$ (a becomes b plus c).

The calculation performed by the computer consists of taking the values of the variables b and c, adding them together and assigning the result as the value of the variable a. The equality sign in the equation is replaced by the symbol := which is interpreted as "becomes" to illustrate the direction which the calculation takes.

In addition to the mathematical content of the language, provision is also made for organisational procedures which are always required. The complete Algol program consists of a series of statements, either organisational or mathematical in content, and the computer carries out the import of these statements in a logical sequence.

The program, when complete, is offered to a computer, possibly by means of paper tape, which has the program punched in coded form on it. This tape is then read as data by a compiler which translates the Algol statements into a language suitable for the particular computer. It is, therefore, possible to obtain from a computer an "object" program which is in the machine code of that computer, and which carries out the calculations required by the original Algol program.

It is unnecessary here for us to consider the implications of programming beyond the stage of producing the Algol program, since subsequent stages depend upon the nature of the computer to be used, and are performed automatically by that computer.

As mentioned earlier, the Algol programmer has on occasions to concern himself with the characteristics of a specific computer. This is always so in the case of organisational statements to input and output data, since different computers have different devices to perform these functions. It is for this reason that the pure Algol language makes no provision for input and output operations. Each computer has its own statements for this purpose. Other minor variations of the language may occur, particularly in the case of small computers which may only permit the use of a subset of the full Algol facilities. Such a restriction does not prevent the programmer performing some types of calculation, but merely makes the program more cumbersome.

The version of Algol used in this book is that acceptable to an Elliott 803 computer. This version should be acceptable to most computers having an Algol compiler with the exception of the input and output statements which may, of course, be different in each case.

1.2 Programming procedure : Flow diagrams

Before attempting to write a program, the steps of the calculation to be performed may usefully be set out in the form of a flow diagram.

To take a simple example, a flow diagram describing

INTRODUCTION

a method for calculating the average of ten numbers could look as below:

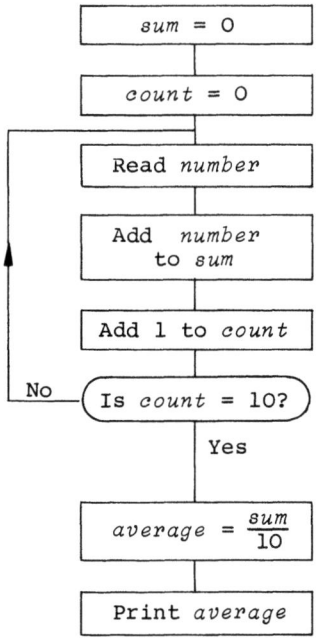

Such a logical diagram indicates the steps required to obtain the result. It can clearly be seen that some of the steps are purely organisational, that is those concerned with the count, and these would correspond to the organisational statements of the Algol program produced from this flow diagram.

The more complicated the calculations become, the more essential is the requirement for a flow diagram, not only to clarify the logical thinking of the programmer but also to enable a third party to gain a quicker grasp of the essentials of the problem, possibly with a view to subsequent modification.

1.3 The Algol program

A complete Algol program written for an Elliott

803 computer according to the flow diagram in 1.2 would be:

Average of ten numbers;

 begin
   real *number, sum, average;*
   integer *count;*
   switch *s*:=*repeat;*
   sum:=0·0;
   count:=0;
repeat:**read** *number;*
   sum:=sum+number;
   count:=count+1;
   if *count≠10* **then** **goto** *repeat;*
   average:=sum/10·0;
   print *average*
 end;

  This program would be supplied to the computer for compilation together with ten numbers which would be looked at when the compiled program was executed. The printed result of the calculation would afterwards be returned to the user.

2

FUNDAMENTALS OF ALGOL

2.1 Introduction

Having seen in the previous chapter an example of the form taken by a complete Algol program, we shall now proceed to consider in some detail the basic elements of Algol programming.

2.2 Identifiers and Numbers

In Algol, a variable is referred to by a name. This name is chosen by the programmer and is called an 'identifier'. Identifiers may be any sequence of letters of the alphabet (upper or lower case) and digits (0-9) starting with a letter.

In the example of Section 1.3 the programmer chose the names *number*, *sum*, *average* and *count* to be the identifiers.

Normal signed or unsigned decimal numbers may be written as numerical constants in an Algol program, or for data.

Use of decimal integer exponents is permitted and these are written with the base 10 inserted below the line.

The general form of a number is

(sign)(integer part)(·fractional part)($_{10}$(sign)exponent)

where the contents of any pair of brackets may be omitted.

Thus the following are examples of valid forms:

19,   +123·45,   -·987,   2·57$_{10}$6, $_{10}$-8.

Numbers and variables denoting numbers in an Algol program are divided into two types, namely type <u>integer</u> referring to whole numbers, and type <u>real</u> which refers to any allowed form of number, held to a precision of so many significant figures.

All variables in a program must be classified as

either real or integer depending on which type of number they denote. This is achieved by including all identifiers in declaration lists preceded by the words integer and real, at the head of the program. The order of these declarations is immaterial. The items of a list are separated by commas and terminated by a semicolon.

In the program in Section 1.3 it will be seen that the variable *count* takes only the values 0,1,2 up to 10, and therefore may be regarded as of type integer. On the other hand, the variables *number*, *sum* and *average* may be required to assume values other than whole numbers and so are in the category real.

2.3 Simple arithmetic expressions

One of the most useful features of Algol is that complicated arithmetic expressions involving numerical variables and constants can be written using the operators + - × / and the bracket-pair (and), all of which have their normal mathematical meanings. To overcome typographical difficulties, another operator ↑ is introduced to allow for exponentiation or for powers of variables - the base precedes the symbol ↑ and the exponent or power follows.

For example, the Algol expression

$(a + 2 \times b - 3 \times c) \times d \uparrow 4 \cdot 5 + 6/e$

is the equivalent in normal mathematical notation of

$(a + 2b - 3c)d^{4 \cdot 5} + \frac{6}{e}$.

The division operator / may be used with either type of operand and gives a result of type real. A further division operator ÷ may only be used for operands of type integer and produces a result of type integer by ignoring any fractional part if necessary.

The order of execution of arithmetic operations is from left to right in the expression, unless the next operation has a higher priority according to the list:

    1. ↑
    2. × / ÷
    3. + -   .

This order can be over-ridden by the normal use of brackets.

In an Algol arithmetic expression, identifiers,

numbers and bracketed expressions must always be separated from each other by one of the arithmetic operation symbols, and no two of these symbols may be adjacent. For instance,

a^{-b} is written in Algol as $a\uparrow(-b)$.

2.4 Standard functions

Algol reserves a set of identifiers for some standard functions which perform processes frequently required. These may be inserted into arithmetic expressions in the same way as ordinary variables.

The list of functions available and their definitions (where AE stands for arithmetic expression) is:

abs(AE)	for the absolute value (modulus) of the value of the arithmetic expression AE
sqrt(AE)	for the positive square root of AE
sin(AE)	for the sine of AE radians
cos(AE)	for the cosine of AE radians
arctan(AE)	for the principal value (in the range $-\pi/2$ to $+\pi/2$) in radians of the arctangent of the value of AE
ln(AE)	for the natural logarithm (to base e) of the value of AE
exp(AE)	for the exponential function of the value of AE
entier(AE)	for the largest integer not greater than the value of AE

sign(AE)	has the value +1 for AE > 0
	                  0 for AE = 0
	                 -1 for AE < 0.

The brackets around the arithmetic expression are essential in order to avoid ambiguity.

2.5 Assignment statements

The steps in a computation are performed by following statements in an order determined by the programmer.

The most basic form of statement is the assignment statement. The special symbol := which may be read as 'becomes' or 'is assigned the value of' is

used. Only a single identifier can appear to the left of the sign. The right-hand side of the statement consists of an arithmetic expression involving numbers and identifiers which have already been assigned values. The action called for by an assignment statement is that the value of the expression on the right-hand side should be computed and then assigned to the variable on the left-hand side of the symbol :=.
For example, the statements

$$a := 4 \cdot 52;$$
$$b := a + 2 \cdot 46;$$

would cause the variable called a to take the value 4·52, and then the variable called b to take the value equal to the sum of the current value of a, namely 4·52, and 2·46, that is 6·98.

Statements must be separated from each other by semicolons.

It is possible to extend the left-hand side by writing a list of variables of the same type with assignment symbols separating them. The value of the expression is then assigned to all the left-hand variables.

For example, the statement

$$c := d := a \times b;$$

would assign the value of the product of the values of a and b to both the variables d and c.

It is allowable to have an arithmetic expression differing in type from a variable to which it is assigned. In this event, conversion is automatic, <u>real</u> expressions assigned to <u>integer</u> variables being rounded to the nearest integer.

2.6 Simple input and output statements

To produce Algol programs of practical value it is necessary to be able to produce results in a usable form and possibly to set program variables initially.

The input-output statements described below refer specifically to Elliott 803 Algol.

The statement

<u>read</u> a;

has the effect of putting the variable, with identifier a, equal in value to a number read from a data stream. It also has the effect of making the position in the data stream move on one number in readiness for the next read instruction.

The **read** statement may be extended to read more than one number by supplying a list of identifiers to be assigned the values of the numbers.

For example, the statement

        read $a,b,c;$

would assign the next three numbers in the data stream to the variables a, b and c respectively.

The output statement

        print $a,b,c;$

operates in a similar manner to the read statement, the value of each variable in the list being produced on a new line in a standard format.

2.7 Complete program

Before a group of statements becomes a program, it must be bracketed at the beginning and end by the words **begin** and **end**. The underlining indicates that these words are Algol basic symbols with a function, and not just a sequence of letters. The types of all the identifiers of variables which occur in the program must be indicated by declarations at the head of the program, immediately after the word **begin**.

Finally, for the Elliott 803 computer, a program title should be inserted before the initial **begin** and a semicolon after the final **end**. The title may consist of any characters terminated by a semicolon.

The following complete small program would read the value of the area of a circle and print its radius.

Radius of a circle;

begin
    real *area, radius;*
    read *area;*
    radius:=sqrt(area/3·14159);
    print *radius*
end;

It should be noted that an appropriate approximation for π must be used as a constant.

2.8 Labels and goto statements

The normal sequential execution of statements may be interrupted by a **goto** statement of the form goto *label;*.

The label may be any identifier not used for some other purpose and must prefix a statement, separated from it by a colon thus:

label: *statement;*.

An illustration is given in Section 1.3 by

repeat: read *number;*.

The goto statement has the effect of making the labelled statement the next in sequence.

Elliott 803 Algol demands that all labels used in a program must be declared in the form of a switch. An example of a switch declaration is

switch $s:=L1,L2,L3;$

where s is the switch identifier and $L1,L2,L3$ are labels occurring in the program.

2.9 Conditional statements

Conditional statements in Algol begin with the symbol if and hence are often called if statements. The simple form of an if statement is

if *relationship* then *statement;*

where the relationship consists of two arithmetic expressions separated by one of the symbols $= \neq < \leq > \geq$, each of which has the normal mathematical meaning.

An example is

if $d \neq 0$ then $f:=n/d;$.

If the relationship part of an if statement is true then the statement following the symbol then will be performed, otherwise this statement will be ignored, and the next in sequence will be considered.

The statement part of an if statement need not be an assignment statement as in the example above. A very useful form is achieved by incorporating a goto statement: for example,

if $b\uparrow2 < 4 \times a \times c$ then goto *complex;*

where *complex* is a label.

A more powerful form of conditional statement is made possible by using the symbol else. The statement

if *relationship* then *statement 1* else *statement 2;*

will obey '*statement 1*' if the relationship is true,

otherwise it will obey '*statement 2*'. For example,

   if $d \neq 0$ **then** $f:=n/d$ **else** $f:=0;$

will evaluate f as the quotient n/d if d is non-zero
or it will assign f the value zero if d is zero.
   This form of a conditional statement will even
allow conditional statements to appear within it, but
only in the position after **else**. Only unconditional
statements may appear in the position of '*statement 1*'.
The combination '**then if**' is not allowed.

2.10 Elementary **for** statements

   It is often necessary to repeat a calculation a
number of times. For instance, a program to produce
the cubes of ten numbers would perform the same operation ten times, but with ten different values. These
operations could be achieved by a sequence of assignment statements, but a more economical and elegant
form of expression is the **for** statement.
   A very simple example of a common type of usage
is

   for $i:=1$ **step** 1 **until** 20 **do** **print** $i;$.

This statement takes an initial value of i as 1. If
the value of i does not exceed the upper limit, 20,
the statement **print** i is carried out. The value of i
is increased by the step size, 1, and the process is
repeated until the upper limit is exceeded. The effect
of the complete **for** statement is that the integers 1
to 20 are printed.
   The initial value, the step size and the upper
limit may all be arithmetic expressions. The symbol
do is always followed by a statement.
   An alternative type of **for** statement is used
where the calculation is to be repeated with unequal
steps of the controlled variable, and is exemplified
by

   for $f:=0,5,25,26$ **do** $s:=a/(1-r)-f \times s;$.

   In this case the value of s is determined succes-
sively for the values of f in the order in which they
are given in the list. These values may themselves be
replaced by arithmetic expressions, as in

   for $f:=0, r \uparrow n$ **do** $s:=a/(1-r)-f \times s;$.

   The form of a **for** statement may thus be summar-
ised as:

for controlled variable:=*FLE,FLE,...,FLE* do *statement;*

where *FLE* stands for '*for* list element'.
The for list gives a sequence of values which are consecutively assigned to the controlled variable before each execution of the statement following do.
We have described here two forms taken by a for list element, delaying consideration of the third type until Chapter 7.
It should be noted that the controlled variable which has been given the values of the for list elements has no specified value at the completion of the for statement. Exits from within a for statement by means of a goto statement in the statement following do are allowed. In such an event the controlled variable keeps its current value on exit.
The use of a for statement within an if statement is restricted in that it must not be followed by else.

2.11 Compound statements

In Algol, statements may be grouped together to make a block or compound statement by enclosing a sequence of one or more statements in the statement brackets begin and end. The sequence of statements is then treated as one whole.
The symbol end can be considered as a dummy statement and can be labelled. Further, the semicolon terminating a statement may be omitted provided that it is followed immediately by the symbol end.
The restrictions on the use of if statements, and for statements within if statements, may be overcome by enclosing the offending statement by begin and end, thus making it a compound statement on which there are no restrictions.

2.12 Example program

A possible program to solve the set of quadratic equations,

$$x^2 + ax + 1 = 0$$

for a taking all whole number values from 2 to 50 is given below.
The program illustrates the use of a compound statement within a for statement.

FUNDAMENTALS OF ALGOL   13

Solution of a set of quadratic equations;
begin
    integer a;
    real x1,x2,f;
    for a:=2 step 1 until 50 do
    begin
        f:=sqrt(a↑2-4);
        x1:=(-a+f)/2;
        x2:=(-a-f)/2;
        print x1,x2
    end
end;

The square root is calculated and assigned to f in order to avoid repetition of the same square root procedure, effecting an economy both in writing and execution time.

2.13 Subscripted variables and arrays

It is often necessary to perform the same operations on many different sets of data. When this is the case it is convenient to be able to allocate a single name or identifier to groups of data and distinguish between individual items by means of subscripts.

In Algol, an identifier which carries one or more subscripts is known as an array, and an array element thus takes the form

$$identifier\ [i,j,k,...]$$

where i,j,k are integer subscripts.

Subscripted variables may be either of type **real** or **integer**. They must be declared at the head of a block of program by a declaration of the form:

    (**real**) **array** identifier [l:u, l:u, ...],....,
                   identifier [l:u, l:u, ...];

or **integer array** ...;

where l and u are the lower and upper limits of each subscript of the array.

If no type symbol appears in the declaration then the elements of the array are understood to be **real**.

Subscripted variables may be used in arithmetic expressions in the same way as ordinary variables. The subscripts themselves may be arithmetic expressions.

3

SORTING NUMBERS

3.1 A simple sorting problem

If there are available 100 numbers, not arranged in any order of magnitude, we can sort them into ascending order by a computer method.

A very elementary approach to this problem is to compare it with the 'chess ladder' technique employed in many chess clubs. The principle is to list the players in any order of ability. Any two players occupying neighbouring positions in the ladder may play each other, the winning player consequently taking over the upper position of the pair.

If this technique is adapted to the problem of sorting numbers, the numbers would be arranged as a list, and all consecutive pairs examined until the final 'ladder' positions were achieved. The criterion for the actual comparison of each pair would be that the smaller numbers would occupy the upper position.

3.2 A basic sorting program

Let us presume that the 100 numbers to be sorted are available as a data stream. Clearly the first step is to accept these values as they occur and to arrange them as elements of a one dimensional array (to all intents and purposes a list), which is identified by the name *number*.

Once they are so arranged the comparisons of the pairs of values may commence. The logical interpretation would be:

'Compare one element with the next lower one in the list; if the upper one is the larger, they must be interchanged; otherwise they must be left alone'.

SORTING NUMBERS

In Algol this is stated by the following:

<u>if</u> *number* [*i*]>*number* [*i*+1] <u>then</u>
<u>begin</u>
    store:=*number*[*i*+1];
    number [*i*+1] :=*number* [*i*];
    number [*i*] :=*store*
<u>end</u>;

This statement becomes the heart of the program.
The remaining part of the program must ensure that all the necessary comparisons have occurred. One way is to start with the first pair, that is, *number* [1] and *number* [2] and after dealing with them, the second pair of *number* [2] and *number* [3] and so on until *number* [99] and *number* [100] are compared. After the first complete pass through the array, the largest element must be in the last position in the array.

In the worst possible case, the smallest number is initially the last element in the array, and on the first pass through the array will have advanced only one place. Thus 99 passes through the array are necessary to ensure that all sorting has taken place. The flow diagram illustrating the technique is given in Figure 3/1.

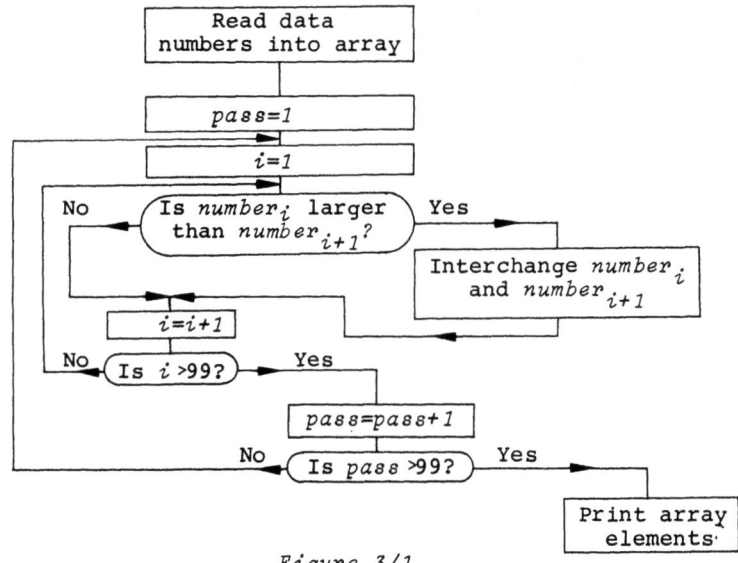

Figure 3/1

16 PROGRAMMING BY CASE STUDIES

Sort 100 numbers (1st method);
```
begin
      integer pass,i;
      real store;
      array number [1:100];
      for i:=1 step 1 until 100 do read number [i];
      for pass:=1 step 1 until 99 do
      begin
            for i:=1 step 1 until 99 do
            begin
                  if number [i] >number [i+1] then
                  begin
                        store:=number [i+1];
                        number [i+1]:=number [i];
                        number [i]:=store
                  end
            end
      end
      for i:=1 step 1 until 100 do print number[i]
end;
```

3.3 A more efficient version

The above is the simplest and least sophisticated program which could probably be written. However, programming is an art, and a programmer will inevitably want to add some measure of finesse to his product.

Immediately, two criticisms may be made. Firstly, some of the begin and end symbols are redundant, and secondly, it is not necessary to make a complete pass through the array every time. Thus a programmer with a little experience would write the program set out below.

Sort 100 numbers (1st method, improved);
```
begin
      integer pass,i;
      real store;
      array number [1:100];
      for i:=1 step 1 until 100 do read number[i];
      for pass:=1 step 1 until 99 do
      for i:=1 step 1 until 100-pass do
      if number [i] >number [i+1] then
      begin
            store:=number [i+1];
            number [i+1]:=number [i];
            number [i]:=store
      end;
      for i:=1 step 1 until 100 do print number [i]
end;
```

3.4 An alternative program

In the first approach to this problem, the emphasis is towards allowing for the worst possible case.

As the experience of the programmer grows, a little more sophistication will be introduced, and the execution of the program will depend on the data. For this problem, a data-dependent program can be readily written.

The previous example ensured that 99 passes through the array were completed, although in all probability, no interchanges of numbers took place in the last so many passes. The approach is changed now so that once a pass occurs with no interchanges, no further passes are necessary.

A new variable, *exchange*, is introduced, having one of two values, 0 or 1.

At the beginning of each pass, the value of *exchange* is made equal to 0. Whenever an interchange of numbers takes place, the value of *exchange* is made equal to 1.

If, at the end of a pass, the value of *exchange* is still equal to 0, then clearly no interchanges have taken place, and the sorting is complete.

The flow diagram for this program is shown in Figure 3/2.

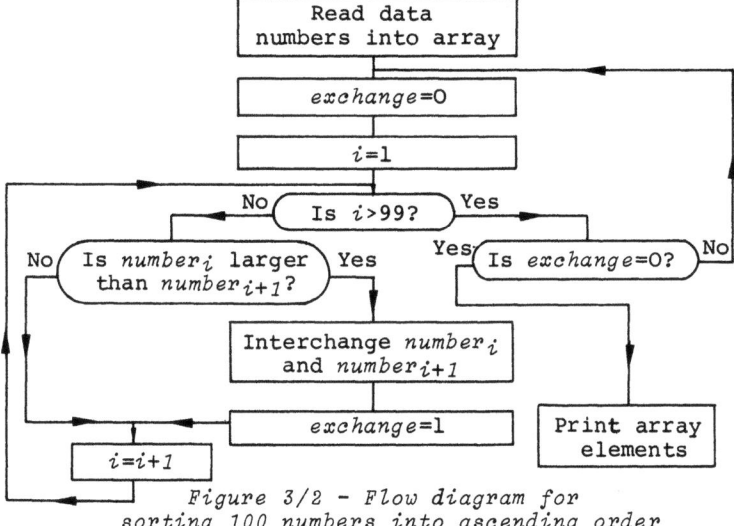

Figure 3/2 - Flow diagram for sorting 100 numbers into ascending order

Sort 100 numbers (2nd method);
<u>begin</u>
    <u>integer</u> *i,exchange;*
    <u>real</u> *store;*
    <u>array</u> *number* [*1:100*];
    <u>switch</u> *s*:=*nextpass;*
    <u>for</u> *i*:=*1* <u>step</u> *1* <u>until</u> *100* <u>do</u> <u>read</u> *number* [*i*];
nextpass:exchange:=*0;*
    <u>for</u> *i*:=*1* <u>step</u> *1* <u>until</u> *99* <u>do</u>
    <u>if</u> *number*[*i*]>*number*[*i+1*] <u>then</u>
    <u>begin</u>
        store:=*number* [*i+1*];
        number [*i+1*]:=*number* [*i*];
        number [*i*]:=*store;*
        exchange:=*1*
    <u>end</u>;
    <u>if</u> *exchange*≠*0* <u>then</u> <u>goto</u> *nextpass;*
    <u>for</u> *i*:=*1* <u>step</u> *1* <u>until</u> *100* <u>do</u> <u>print</u> *number*[*i*]
<u>end</u>;

3.5 Further improvements

The above program ensures that the number of passes is limited only to those necessary. However, each pass is still a full one, with all pairs being checked in each pass. It is desirable to cut down so that only those pairs which are still incorrect are checked.

To do this, the <u>for</u>-loop controlling *i* is dropped, and replaced by a straightforward count on *i*. An upper limit for the pass occurs when *i* reaches 99 initially, and it is reduced on every pass.

Instead of reducing it by 1, as in the first method, it is reduced to the point at which the exchange took place on the previous pass. In fact, it is 1 fewer than the value where that exchange occurred. The variable *exchange* in this program is used to record the value of *i* where the interchange occurred. The *passlimit* value is set at the end of the pass to be 1 fewer than the value of *exchange*.

To determine when all interchanges have occurred, it is possible to test the value of *exchange* to see if it has changed, for it must change in every pass where there is any alteration in the order of the numbers. If it has not changed, then the sorting is complete.

The flow diagram is given in Figure 3/3.

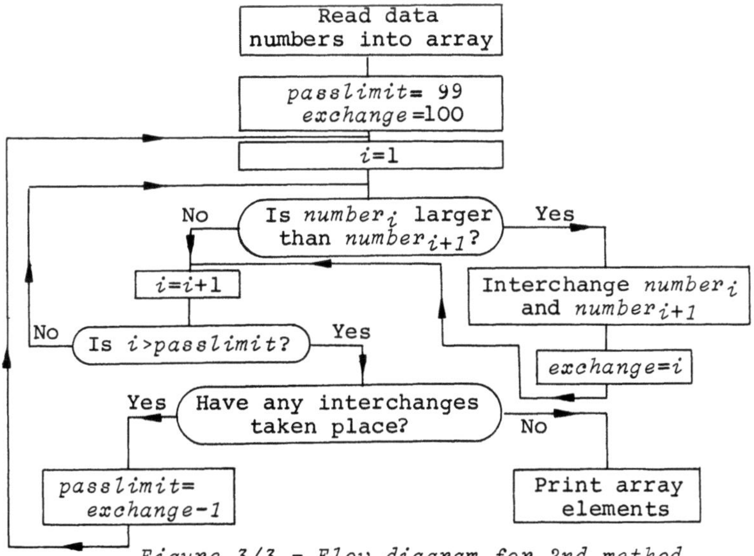

SORTING NUMBERS 19

Figure 3/3 - Flow diagram for 2nd method
(improved) of sorting 100 numbers

Sort 100 numbers (2nd method, improved);
begin
    integer *i,passlimit,exchange;*
    real *store;*
    array *number*$[1:100]$;
    switch *s:=nextpass,comparison;*
    for $i:=1$ **step** 1 **until** 100 **do** **read** *number*$[i]$;
    passlimit:=99; exchange:=100;
nextpass: $i:=1$;
comparison: **if** *number*$[i]$>*number*$[i+1]$ **then**
    begin
        store:=number$[i+1]$; *number*$[i+1]$:=*number*$[i]$
        number$[i]$:=*store; exchange:=i*
    end;
    $i:=i+1$;
    if $i \leq passlimit$ **then goto** *comparison;*
    if *passlimit*≠*exchange-1* **then**
    begin
        passlimit:=exchange-1;
        goto *nextpass*
    end;
    for $i:=1$ **step** 1 **until** 100 **do** **print** *number*$[i]$
end;

4

THE CENTRE OF ENGLAND

4.1 The problem

The traditional 'centre' of England is at Meriden - between Coventry and Birmingham. But what do we mean by the "Centre" of England?

Do we mean the centre of gravity of a set of points representing counties, the county towns, for instance? Should these points at the county towns be weighted by population, or by area, or by some other value? Perhaps we mean the centre of gravity of a plane lamina shaped as the country; - but might we not equally well mean the centre of gravity of a wire shaped as the boundary line and coast?

We can glibly talk about the centre of England, but we might very well have referred to the combination of England and Wales - although it is very likely that most of us would not think of including Scotland in our calculations as well.

Inevitably then, there are many ways of looking at this problem - each of which has a justification. In this chapter we shall select a few of the ways of attacking the problem and present them with their programs and solutions.

Common to all these techniques, however, is the need for geographical reference points. In every case these will be taken as the points of the National Grid System. This is a set of Cartesian coordinates based on kilometre squares with the origin to the southwest of Lands End. Thus every point will have a coordinate east and a coordinate north of this origin.

Population figures refer to the 1961 Census.

4.2.1 The centre of England by county towns

The quickest and easiest way to calculate an approximation to the centre of England is to select all the county towns and to regard them all as a set of weights of equal size.

Thus, we need the values of the grid reference of the county towns. Taunton, for instance, the county town of Somerset, has reference 322 km east and 125 km north of the origin.

To find the centre of gravity, all that needs to be done is for all the east coordinates to be added, and for all the north coordinates to be added, and in each case divided by the number of counties. It is thus easy to arrange our program to read in one coordinate (the easterly one) and follow this by the second coordinate (northerly) for each county town. The program will read numbers in pairs until it gets to the last one. But how will it know whether it has reached the last one?

We could control this by putting the number of counties as a separate number at the front of the data, and let this determine how many pairs of numbers are to be read. But if we want this to be flexible, it is better to terminate the data by a special number which will indicate when the data has been completely read. A suitable such number is -1, since it is quite impossible for this to occur as a coordinate. Thus, when the value -1 is encountered, the data stream has been exhausted, and all the required information has been assembled for the answer to be calculated and printed out.

In tackling this problem we could read all the initial data in the form of an array; however, since we are only using these values once, it is much better to carry out the addition as the values are read, and not to hold them in the computer store any longer than necessary. This is good practice, always to be followed.

The flow diagram is given in Figure 4/1, and a diagram illustrating the scatter of the county towns in Figure 4/2.

FIGURE 4/1.
Flow Diagram for the Centre of England by County Towns.

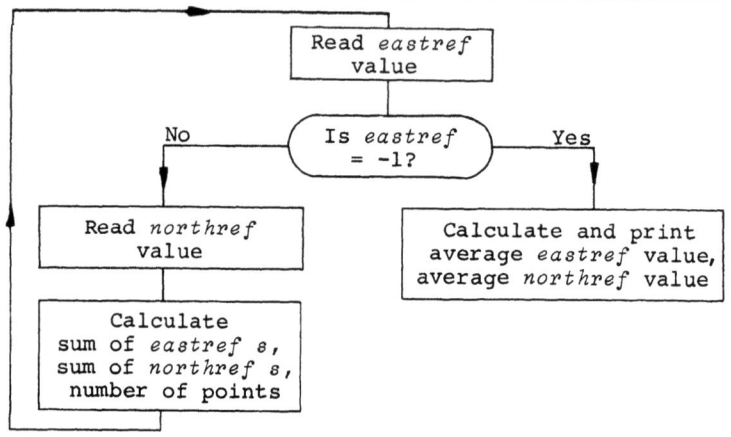

4.2.2 The program

```
Centre of England by county towns;
begin
      real eastref,northref,sumeast,sumnorth,sumweight,
      eastcoord,northcoord;
      switch s:=nextref;
      sumeast:=sumnorth:=sumweight:=0·0;
nextref:read eastref;
      if sign(eastref)≠-1 then
      begin
            read northref;
            sumeast:=sumeast+eastref;
            sumnorth:=sumnorth+northref;
            sumweight:=sumweight+1·0;
            goto nextref
      end;
      eastcoord:=sumeast/sumweight;
      northcoord:=sumnorth/sumweight;
      print eastcoord,northcoord
end;
```

4.2.3 The results

This is basically a very simple problem and could very well be worked out using pencil and paper. However, after taking a number of decisions such as whether Bodmin or Truro should count as the County Town of Cornwall (most reference books still give Bodmin), and whether to count three different county towns in Yorkshire rather than one, a set of coordinates for the centre was achieved.

For England and Wales   415 km east, 276 km north.
For England only   447 km east, 274 km north.

4.2.4 The centre of England by counties, weighted at county towns

In the example above, the technique was simply to evaluate the centre by taking each county town on a par with all the others. However, all the counties are not the same size, nor have they the same populations. Therefore, it would seem much more appropriate if we were to weight the counties either by their populations, or by their areas.

If we take the figures that have already been worked out for the county towns in the way of reference points, we need only to include their areas and their populations and to incorporate either as a simple weighting factor. If the weighting factor is w_i for the ith county, and its east reference is e_i, then all that must be calculated is

$$\frac{\text{the sum of the products of } w_i \times e_i}{\text{the sum of } w_i}$$

4.2.5 The program

This program is so similar to that quoted in section 4.2.3 that no flow diagram will be given, but the program quoted below will show the changes that have been necessary. These changes allow for the reading of an additional value alongside the reference points of the county towns, this value representing the weighting - either population or area - of the county, and also allow for the weight to be brought in as the appropriate factor.

Centre of England weighted at county towns;
<u>begin</u>
    <u>real</u> *eastref,northref,aweight,sumeast,sumnorth,*
         sumweight,eastcoord,northcoord;
    <u>switch</u> *s:=nextref;*
    sumeast:=sumnorth:=sumweight:=0·0
nextref: <u>read</u> *eastref;*
    <u>if</u> *sign(eastref)≠-1* <u>then</u>
    <u>begin</u>
        <u>read</u> *northref,aweight;*
        sumeast:=sumeast+eastref×aweight;
        sumnorth:=sumnorth+northref×aweight,
        sumweight:=sumweight+aweight;
        <u>goto</u> *nextref*
    <u>end</u>;
    eastcoord:=sumeast/sumweight;
    northcoord:=sumnorth/sumweight;
    <u>print</u> *eastcoord,northcoord*
<u>end</u>;

4.2.6 The results

Using the same county towns as previously, and consequently the same coordinates, two further calculations were achieved, for population and area, and in each case for the larger and smaller areas which we are considering.

For England and Wales

	By Area	407 km east, 290 km north
	By Population	454 km east, 274 km north.

For England alone

	By Area	426 km east, 292 km north
	By Population	461 km east, 275 km north.

4.2.7 An appraisal of the programs

So far the programs have required three separate sets of data to be prepared. If we take one look at the data, it should occur to us that, if we had prepared one set of data only, then it would have done for all three sets of results.

This may be done by using the full data, i.e. four values to each county: two reference points, the area, and the population.

In the first program all that is required in the way of modification is for two additional real identifiers to be declared - call them *aweight* and *bweight* - and the second read statement becomes

    read *northref,aweight,bweight;*.

The program will cause four numbers per county to be read into the computer, although the latter two will never appear in the calculation.

The same read statement could be used in the second program, and by keeping the data exactly the same, a third program could be created just by altering the second read statement again to

    read *northref,bweight,aweight;*.

There thus become three similar programs, all using one set of data. By careful planning and consideration of what is to be achieved, unnecessary and tiresome work in data preparation my be omitted.

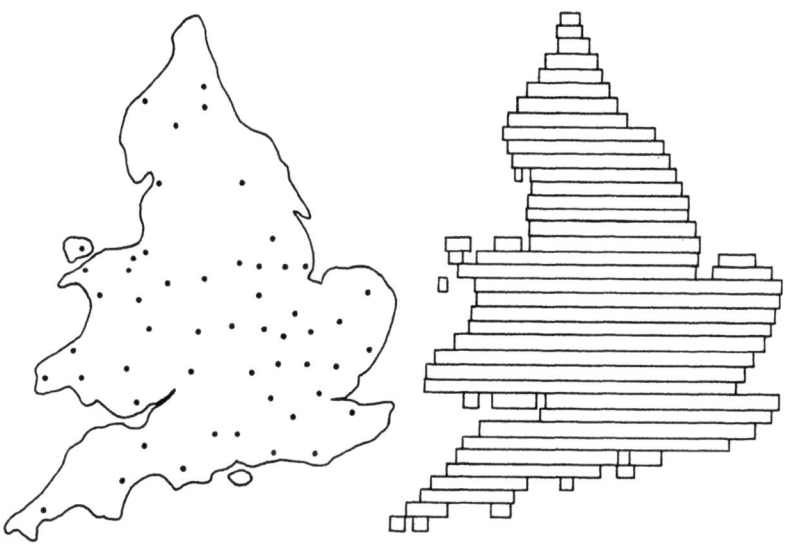

Figure 4/2 - The position of the county towns

Figure 4/3 - Representation of the country as strips of a lamina

4.3.1 The centre of England by strips of a lamina.

It is clearly quite possible to extend the method discussed in the previous section. The country may be divided into strips of equal width, instead of county areas. The weight of each strip is proportional to its length and acts at its midpoint. An outline of this is shown in Figure 4/3.

4.3.2 The collection of data

The collection of data for this example is important - it represents quite a proportion of time taken in map reading. It is important that it is made in a manner which is easy to record, and subsequently prepare for the computer.

With a map of Britain at a scale of about 10 miles to the inch, and overruled with the National Grid System of lines 10 km apart, it is possible to start at the most southerly point, and work along the grid line from east to west, noting (to the nearest kilometre) the coast or boundary line. It is quite clear that there will be at the least two points, and there may be more where the coast is very broken. But, however many points there are, there must be an even number, for we continue along the line until there is no more land to be considered.

Effectively then, our data occur naturally as we prepare them, in the form of one northerly reference point and an even number of easterly reference points, followed by similar information for all the other grid lines going north.

This is the obvious way of preparing our data. But how will the computer detect whether a number which it receives is a northerly or an easterly coordinate?

One way is to divide all the northerly coordinates by 1000, so that they become fractions. Then it is possible each time a number is read into the computer to test it to see whether its value is less than 1; if it is, then it is a northerly coordinate, and can be treated as such, at the same time multiplying by 1000 in order to bring it back to its required level.

Again, as in the previous case, we do not know in advance how many points there will be in the data as a whole: we can again terminate the data by placing the value -1 at the end.

4.3.3 The approach to the program

The method in this case is developed from the previous program, but it is necessary to distinguish between the coordinates. As each observation is read, the program must test it to see whether it is a north coordinate, an east coordinate, or the terminating value.

When a north coordinate is read, it remains as the operative north coordinate, until such time as a new one is read in. The east coordinates occur in pairs, so that when two east values are read in, the mean value of the two indicates the midpoint; the difference between the two indicates the length of the strip. Thus we can easily achieve the north coordinate, the east coordinate, and the size (or weight) of the strip. The remainder of the calculation follows as for the previous example.

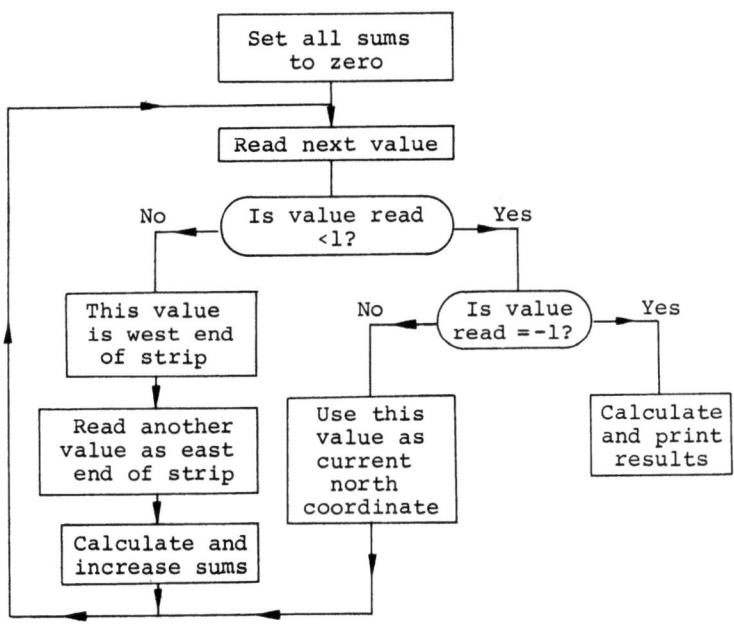

Figure 4/4 - The flow diagram for the laminar approach

4.3.4 The program

```
Centre of England by laminar strips;
begin
      real observation,eastref,northref,weight,sumnorth,
           sumeast,sumweight,oncoast,offcoast,eastcoord,
           northcoord;
      switch s:=answers,nextobservation;
      sumeast:=sumnorth:=sumweight:=0·0;
nextobservation: read observation;
      if observation<1·0 then
      begin
            if observation<0·0 then goto answers;
            northref:=observation×1000·0;
            goto nextobservation
      end;
      oncoast:=observation;
      read offcoast;
      weight:=offcoast-oncoast;
      eastref:=(offcoast+oncoast)× 0·5;
      sumnorth:=sumnorth+northref×weight;
      sumeast:=sumeast+eastref×weight;
      sumweight:=sumweight+weight;
      goto nextobservation;
answers: eastcoord:=sumeast/sumweight;
      northcoord:=sumnorth/sumweight;
      print eastcoord,northcoord
end;
```

4.3.5 The results

On the data collected for strips, 10 km wide, the strips running from east to west, and points measured to 1 km accuracy, the following results were achieved:

for England and Wales   415·0 km east, 292·7 km north.

The additional accuracy of one decimal place is quoted at this point since the data are considerably more accurate than before, and it is interesting to compare it with a further set of results to justify the accuracy.

The country can just as easily be divided into strips of the same width, but in this case running from south to north. If this is done, then the first value quoted on each line is the east coordinate, and this is the one which is divided by 1000 before

feeding to the computer.
Exactly the same program may be used as for the strips in the easterly direction: we must, however, realise the fact that the data which are printed out by the computer will have printed the east coordinate as the northerly one, and vice versa. The computer does not distinguish between them for they are presented purely as a set of figures in a given order, and in this case reversing the order will reverse the order of the results printed.
This is not always the case.
By running this program again the following emerged:

for England and Wales   414·7 km east, 293·3 km north.

By comparing these results with those obtained for the strips in the easterly direction, it will be seen that there is very little difference indeed. They certainly justify presenting to the nearest kilometre.

4.4.1 The centre of England - the wire frame approach

The third technique to be adopted is that of finding the centre of gravity of a wire which has been bent in the shape of the coast or boundary of the country.

The data items in the strips of the lamina approach of the previous program all refer to points on the coast or boundary, and since they have all been measured, and prepared for the computer, then it is reasonable to use these.

The program is similar to the previous one, but in this case we take a unit weight for every coastal point, counting up the total number of points as we go.

As there are two sets of data already prepared, the program can be run for each set.

4.4.2 The program

```
Centre of England by wire frame;
begin
      real observation,northref,sumnorth,sumeast,
           sumweight,eastcoord,northcoord;
      switch s:=answers,nextobservation;
      sumeast:=sumnorth:=sumweight:=0·0;
nextobservation: read observation;
      if observation<1·0 then
      begin
           if observation<0·0 then goto answers;
           northref:=observation×1000·0;
           goto nextobservation
      end;
      sumeast:=sumeast+observation;
      sumnorth:=sumnorth+northref;
      sumweight:=sumweight+1·0;
      goto nextobservation;
answers: eastcoord:=sumeast/sumweight;
      northcoord:=sumnorth/sumweight;
      print eastcoord,northcoord
end;
```

4.4.3 The results

For England and Wales

easterly strips   373·6 km east, 260·3 km north;
northerly strips 360·8 km east, 284·7 km north.

From a casual glance, the figures above appear to show a relatively large discrepancy between strips taken in the two directions. Before, however, one suspects either the data or the program it is advisable to see whether there is any justification for the difference.

The country has a more rugged coastline to the South-west and the inlets run mainly from west to east. This is emphasized by the fact that there are some 270 data points for northerly strips and only 242 for easterly ones. We should therefore expect that easterly strips will give a coordinate of the centre of England in a more easterly position than that obtained for northerly strips. A similar type of argument may be advanced to account for the difference in the north coordinate of the centre.

By referring back to the laminar approach, we find that the wire frame approach gives a centre which

THE CENTRE OF ENGLAND   31

is further west by 50 km or so. Again this is
clearly due to the more rugged coastline on the west
of the country.
    The various points obtained for the centre of
England are shown in Figure 4/6.

Figure 4/6 (Below)

*The various centres
    of England*

<u>Key</u>

. Calculated centres
of England and Wales

+ Centres of towns
and cities in the area

1. Kidderminster
2. Birmingham
3. Meriden
4. Coventry
5. Rugby
6. Warwick
7. Leamington

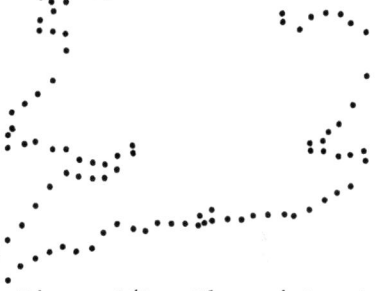

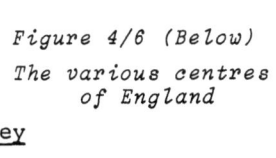

*Figure 4/5 - The points at
the end of northerly strips*

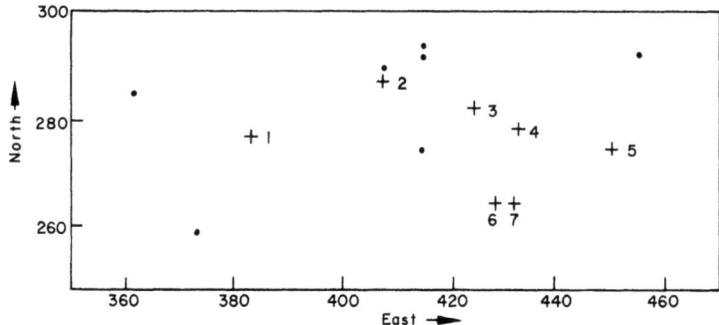

5

EVALUATION OF PI
ACCUMULATION OF INACCURACIES OF ROUND-OFF

5.1 The problem

The problem under consideration is to find an approximation to the value of π (pi) by calculating the numerical summation of the area of a number of strips of a quadrant of a circle radius 2 units. It is required to obtain the greatest possible accuracy.

In fact, this is the very simple problem that many students solve by counting squares on graph paper when they first realise that the area of a circle and the square of the radius are in constant ratio.

5.2 The method

The method which will be taken in this case is that of accumulating the area of the strips which divide up the quadrant of a circle.

There are several methods which may be used to evaluate the area by this general technique:

    (a) Trapezium Rule   (Figure 5/1),
    (b) Mid-ordinate Rule (Figure 5/2),
    (c) Simpson's Rule   (a combination of the above).

For the sake of simplicity, and for the benefit of those who are unfamiliar with it, Simpson's Rule is eliminated from consideration.

It is quite clear from studying the diagrams for the quadrant of a circle that the Mid-ordinate Rule will give a better approximation than the Trapezium Rule, the latter giving a value which is always below the true value. On examination of the diagram for the Mid-ordinate Rule, it will be quite evident that the value obtained will be slightly greater than the true value, but will be much closer to the true value than that obtained for a similar number of strips by the Trapezium Rule. Hence the Mid-ordinate Rule is chosen for this problem.

EVALUATION OF PI

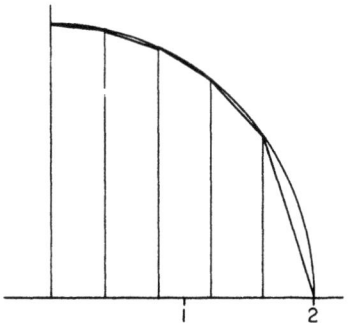

Figure 5/1
Trapezium Rule

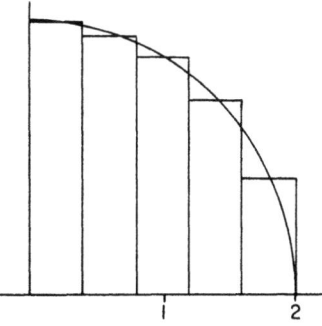

Figure 5/2
Mid-ordinate Rule

5.3 The application of the method

The calculation of the area of each strip depends upon the calculation of ordinates at the mid-point of the strips. If there are n strips, then each strip is $2/n$ wide.

The first ordinate must be evaluated at halfway along that strip, that is, at $1/n$, the second at $3/n$ and so on up to $2 - 1/n$ which is the position along the x-axis of the last ordinate.

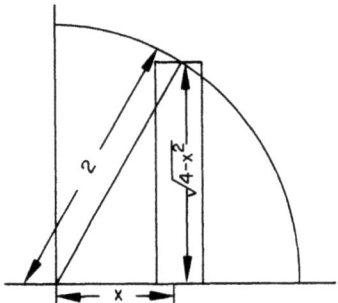

Figure 5/3

If the general position of the ordinate is at x along the x-axis, then the height, y, of that ordinate is given by (Figure 5/3)

$$y = \sqrt{4 - x^2}.$$

Thus we have the core of the program given by

```
sumy:=0·0;
for x:=1/n step 2/n until 2-1/n do
begin
    y:=sqrt(4·0-x↑2);
    sumy:=sumy+y
end;
```

where all the ordinates are added into $sumy$.

On the face of it, the program exists and is trivial by nature. But is it correct?

Suppose one had a computer which worked to 2 decimal places accuracy, and the case of $n = 7$ is considered. The for statement is now understood by the computer as

for $x:=\cdot 14$ step $\cdot 29$ until $2-\cdot 14$ do ...;

since every fractional value is rounded off to 2 decimal places accuracy.

Thus the computer would carry out the calculation controlled by the for statement for values of x of ·14, ·43, ·72, 1·01, 1·30 and 1·59. The next value which the computer should consider would be 1·88 - but as this is above the upper limit of 1·86 specified in the for statement it will not be included in the calculation.

More important, the error incorporated by this omission would be a small one since it will relate to the last ordinate of the seven, and could easily go unnoticed in some calculations. A better version of this statement would be

for $x:=1/n$ step $2/n$ until 2 do ...;

which would be more likely to include all the ordinates, but quite clearly when the number of strips gets very large, there may still be a chance of an overall error arising due to accumulation of individual round-off errors.

An alternative approach is therefore needed, and this can be achieved by using an integer variable, p, to control the number of strips, and calculating the x value from the value of p.

```
sumy:=0·0;
for p:=1 step 2 until n+n-1 do
begin
      x:=p/n;
      y:=sqrt(4·0-x↑2);
      sumy:=sumy+y
end;
```

5.4 The accuracy of the calculation

Having achieved a satisfactory core to the program, the desired accuracy must be achieved. In order to investigate this, the first step is to obtain values of the area for various numbers of strips.

We encompass the basic sequence of statements within another for statement which calls for calculations to be made at various numbers of strips, these numbers being controlled by three values given to the computer as data.

5.5 The program

```
Evaluation of pi by mid-ordinate rule;
begin
      real x,y,sumy,pi;
      integer n,p,lowerlimit,upperlimit,interval;
      read lowerlimit,interval,upperlimit;
      for n:=lowerlimit step interval until
      upperlimit do
      begin
            sumy:=0·0;
            for p:=1 step 2 until n+n-1 do
            begin
                  x:=p/n;
                  y:=sqrt(4·0-x↑2);
                  sumy:=sumy+y
            end;
            pi:=sumy×2·0/n;
            print n,pi
      end
end;
```

5.6 The results

The first trial of the technique was carried out using two different programs, the first one being that outlined in 5.3 and the second that outlined in 5.5, in each case obtaining values for strips from 10 up to 100 in steps of 10.

Number of Strips	Program in 5.3	Program in 5.5
10	3·0275115	3·1524115
20	3·1009896	3·1454306
30	3·1194425	3·1436841
40	3·1429519	3·1429519
50	3·1425656	3·1435655
60	3·1423329	3·1423329
70	3·1421803	3·1421802
80	3·1420737	3·1420736
90	3·1419959	3·1419957
100	3·1379417	3·1419368

A study of these results shows that 4 values in the first 10 of the 5.3 method have one ordinate missing.

Of the remaining 6, only the value for 40 strips is the same for both programs. In all other cases, program 5.5 gives a slightly more accurate value. This is again as a result of the fact that the computer will not hold values other than integers completely accurately.

If these values achieved by program 5.5 are plotted on a graph, a curve clearly converging to the known value of pi will be apparent (Figure 5/4).

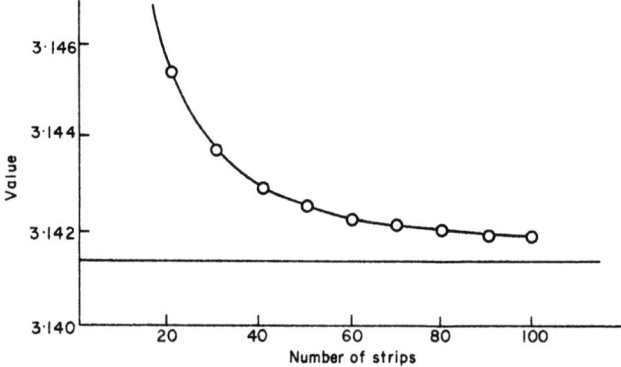

Figure 5/4 - Graph showing improved values of π with low numbers of strips

EVALUATION OF PI

When the calculation was repeated for large numbers of strips, the following results were achieved.

Number of Strips	Value obtained
1000	3·1416034
1200	3·1416010
1400	3·1415991
1600	3·1415981
1800	3·1415972
2000	3·1415962
2200	3·1415963
2400	3·1415957
2600	3·1415953
2800	3·1415952

These results demonstrate that the inaccuracies due to round-off are at the stage of dominating and overriding any increased accuracy due to taking more strips. The value obtained for 2200 strips is actually larger than 2000 strips (Figure 5/5).

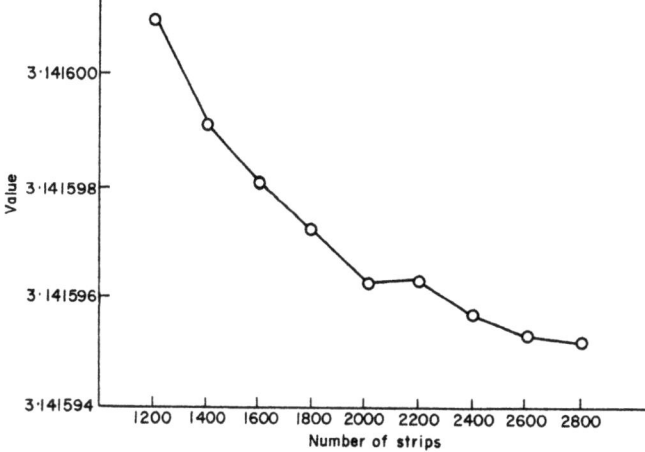

Figure 5/5 - Graph showing that values for π do not necessarily improve with higher numbers of strips

5.7 Review of the program

Whilst we now have a program which produces the desired answers, this program takes time for the computer to execute; when the number of strips gets large - of the order of 1,000 or more, this time is measurable in seconds. For instance, to evaluate pi using 1,000 strips takes 126 seconds of computer time if the program set out in 5.5 is used. On this basis, to evaluate pi for 1,000 to 2,800 strips in intervals of 200 would take 4,788 seconds. It is, therefore, desirable always to be alert to ways of reducing the time spent by a computer - or more precisely, of avoiding unnecessary calculation.

In this program there is a central group of three statements which are continually obeyed for every strip:

$$x:=p/n;$$
$$y:=sqrt(4 \cdot 0-x \uparrow 2);$$
$$sumy:=sumy+y;$$

Quite clearly, if there is to be any reduction in the time taken by the computer over this problem it is going to occur within these three statements.

Whenever an expression, or part of an expression, of the form $x \uparrow 2$ is encountered, the computer will calculate the logarithm of x, multiply it by 2, and then find the antilogarithm of the result. Since this is done in logarithms to base e, this means that $x \uparrow 2$ is normally interpreted by the computer as

$$exp(2 \times ln(x)).$$

Whilst working out values by hand methods it may be appropriate to use logarithms in this way; it is not so with computers. $x \times x$ is performed faster than $x \uparrow 2$, and also $x \times x \times x$ is performed faster than $x \uparrow 3$, but advantages in higher powers of x will depend upon the computer used.

In this case, we can substitute $x \times x$ for $x \uparrow 2$ in the program and expect a reduction in the time taken.

In addition, a further saving in time may be achieved by changing the <u>for</u> statement

<u>for</u> $p:=1$ <u>step</u> 1 <u>until</u> $n+n-1$ <u>do</u> ...;

to the pair of statements

$q:=n+n-1;$
<u>for</u> $p:=1$ <u>step</u> 1 <u>until</u> q <u>do</u> ...;

EVALUATION OF PI

 This technique ensures that the upper limiting value q for the controlled variable p is calculated once only for every summation, and not for every strip.

 The amended program for 1,000 strips occupied only 104 seconds of computer time.

 A saving of 22 seconds in 126 may not seem very important, but if the program were run for the larger problem, the total time drops back to 3951 seconds. Now the saving becomes about 14 minutes in an hour and a quarter. This saving is now worth-while; and as a side issue, it is more accurate for the computer to multiply two numbers together, than to go through the process of taking logarithms and exponentials.

 If the whole emphasis had been on the saving of time, the area could be divided into 2^n strips (for some n), and the number of strips doubled each time around the loop. Half of the ordinates would then already have been calculated for each increase in n, and would not need recalculation. The time taken varies as $\log_2 n$ and not as n.

6
MOVEMENTS IN A SHARE PRICE INDEX

6.1 The problem

Speculative investors in stocks and shares have one main aim; to buy at a low price and to sell at a higher one. It is possible to invest, wait for a $y\%$ rise, then sell; additionally, one may wait for an $x\%$ fall from the present price before buying. Given 500 values of a financial index, can we find the most profitable combinations of $y\%$ rise and $x\%$ fall?

The assumption is that there is £100 available to invest at the start of the index; the investment must be realised on the last of the 500 days at the latest.

The data which are available are typical of a financial index. The starting and finishing values are virtually identical so that the rises and falls in any investment pattern may be taken relative to a constant investment.

Figure 6/1 shows the way that investment may take advantage of rises and falls in the index value.

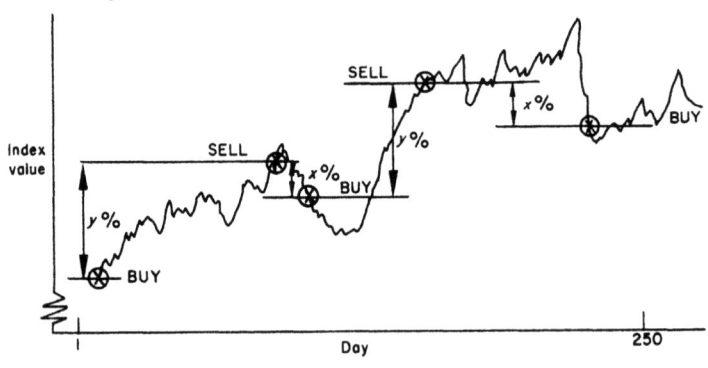

Figure 6/1

6.2 Approach to the problem

The approach to the problem is clear: all 500 values must be read into the computer first. Once they are in the computer store, they may be investigated with all possible arrangements of rises and falls - say 1%, 2% up to 10% for both rise and fall. This means 100 evaluations of performance each over 500 days.

To be completely definitive, we will assume that any purchasing or selling occurs while the index is at that point - that is, there is no delay for the transaction to be completed. We will also assume that there are no transaction charges.

The final print-out is envisaged in the form of a table with the rises in one direction (down the page) and the falls in the other (across the page). Thus it will be possible to find where the better area of investment policy lies, since it will probably be unrealistic to name any one particular value.

The print-out of the problem can refer to the particular rises (or falls) in percentages of the initial investment.

6.3 The method

The flow diagram for this particular problem is shown in figure 6/2.

After the 500 values have been read in, the controls on the rise before selling and the fall before buying are shown as fractions and not as percentages. However, it is assumed that the first purchase is made on the first day with the initial investment of £100.

The second day is then investigated to see whether the necessary rise has occurred for the selling criterion. If it has not, the day counter is increased by one until that criterion is satisfied - or in the extreme case when day 500 has been reached without the selling criterion having been achieved. In either case, the investment is realised (though in separate parts of the program).

Provided that the 500th day has not been reached, there can now be a search for the next buying day. The method is, of course, similar to that for the selling price search, but the buying price depends upon the selling price of the previous transaction, which must therefore have been recorded at that time.

The buying price when reached is recorded, and the whole process is repeated until the time that the

PROGRAMMING BY CASE STUDIES

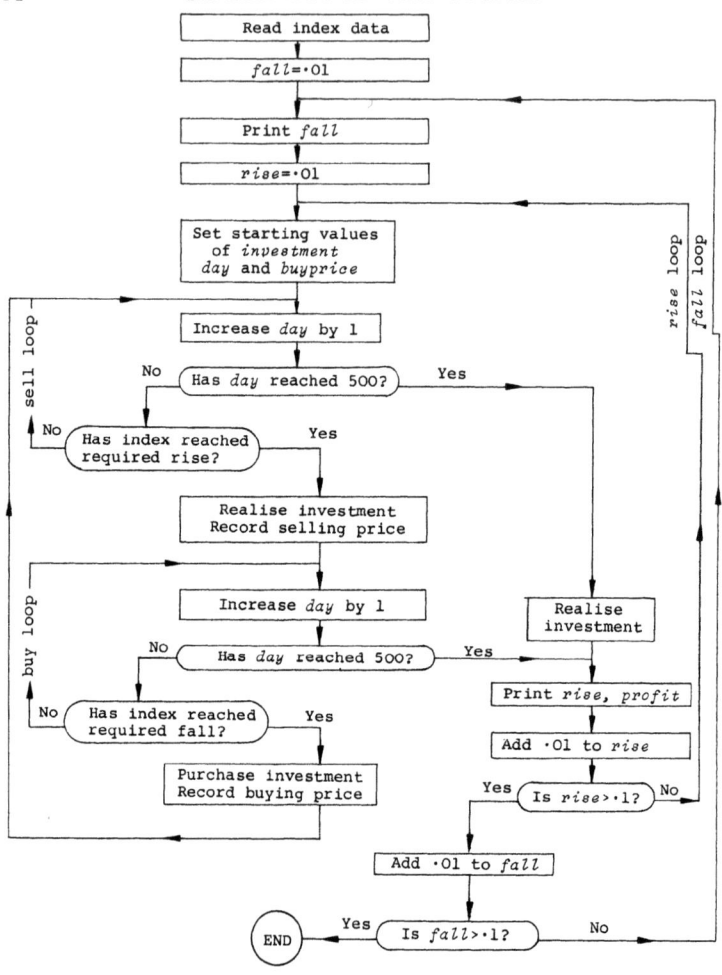

Figure 6/2 - Flow Diagram

MOVEMENTS IN A SHARE PRICE INDEX 43

500 days are accounted for. At this stage the present value of the initial investment must be considered and printed out. Thus, if stock is held on the 500th day, it must, in effect, be realised before this evaluation occurs. By subtracting the initial investment of £100, the profit (or loss) may be realistically shown.

6.4 The program

```
Investment analysis;
begin
      real investment,rise,fall,buyprice,sellprice,
            profit;
      integer day;
      array index [1:500];
      switch s:=sellloop,buyloop,realise,uncash;
      for day:=1 step 1 until 500 do read index[day];
      for fall:=·01 step ·01 until ·105 do
      begin
            print fall;
            for rise:=·01 step ·01 until ·105 do
            begin
                  investment:=100·0;
                  day:=1;
                  buyprice:=index[1];
    sellloop:day:=day+1;
                  if day>499 then goto realise;
                  if index[day]<(1·0+rise)×buyprice then
                  goto sellloop;
                  sellprice:=index[day];
                  investment:=investment×sellprice/buyprice;
     buyloop:day:=day+1;
                  if day>499 then goto uncash;
                  if index[day]>(1·0-fall)×sellprice then
                  goto buyloop;
                  buyprice:=index[day];
                  goto sellloop;
     realise:investment:=investment×index[500]/buyprice;
     uncash:profit:=investment-100·0;
                  print rise,profit
            end
      end
end;
```

6.5 Program appraisal

The program which has been described in 6.4 will of course work - and produce the required answers. It is, however, desirable always to check the program to ensure that the time taken is reduced as much as possible.

If the flow diagram - or the program - is considered, then it is obvious that most of the time will be taken up by either the buying loop or the selling loop. Between them they are traversed 500 times for each combination of rise and fall percentages, a total of 50,000 traverses of a section of program.

The two groups of statements in the inner loops are similar; and there is little we can do to speed up adding 1, or checking whether day 500 has yet been reached. This leaves only the comparison to see if the required level of the index has yet been reached - and, on the face of it, this is the only way it can be stated.

However, if we were doing this problem by hand, then we should not calculate $(1\cdot0+rise) \times buyprice$ every time we compared it with a day's index to see if it had reached the required level. We should calculate $(1\cdot0+rise) \times buyprice$ - and call it, say *criterion* and then compare the value of *criterion* against successive days' values of the index. We should not do all that unncessary calculation ourselves, why should we make the computer?

To implement the change, all that needs to be done, with the additional declaration, is to insert

$$criterion := (1\cdot0+rise) \times buyprice;$$

immediately preceding the *sellloop* label, and change the **if** statement to

if $index[day] < criterion$ **then**

and similarly with the *buyloop*.

The time taken for the program to run on the computer in its original form was reduced from about 29¼ minutes to about 22 minutes in its revised form: over 7 minutes would have been taken asking the computer to repeat calculations that it had already made.

6.6 Results and comments

From a computer run on a set of 500 consecutive values the results achieved are shown below.

MOVEMENTS IN A SHARE PRICE INDEX 45

PROFIT ACHIEVED
Falls %

	1	2	3	4	5	6	7	8	9	10
1	7·9	5·9	6·1	7·8	5·3	4·4	3·6	2·3	2·7	2·6
2	12·6	9·6	14·6	9·7	7·3	7·4	7·8	7·9	5·5	5·1
3	21·7	13·8	13·4	13·6	14·3	10·6	10·2	9·7	10·8	6·4
4	43·3	17·7	17·6	13·1	18·7	13·7	13·0	14·7	13·1	13·3
5	44·1	22·9	15·9	16·2	16·8	23·3	17·4	17·1	16·0	16·2
6	20·9	20·1	12·9	12·9	19·9	12·9	12·9	13·2	13·1	12·8
7	15·0	23·5	23·6	15·2	15·2	14·7	14·7	14·7	14·8	14·9
8	31·6	17·2	17·1	17·1	17·6	17·6	17·2	17·5	17·5	17·2
9	19·1	19·9	19·1	19·1	19·3	19·3	19·3	19·1	19·4	19·4
10	30·1	21·9	22·7	22·4	21·9	22·0	22·0	22·0	22·2	21·9

(Rises %)

Of course, for practical purposes, it is necessary to know the number of transactions which have taken place for each combination of rise and fall, for each transaction in practice represents a charge. In the above case, the program was modified so that these were recorded at the same time, and are shown below.

NUMBER OF TRANSACTIONS
Falls %

	1	2	3	4	5	6	7	8	9	10
1	6	4	5	5	4	3	3	2	2	2
2	5	4	6	4	3	3	3	3	2	2
3	6	4	4	4	4	3	3	3	3	2
4	9	4	4	3	4	3	3	3	3	3
5	8	4	3	3	3	4	3	3	3	3
6	3	3	2	2	3	2	2	2	2	2
7	2	3	3	2	2	2	2	2	2	2
8	4	2	2	2	2	2	2	2	2	2
9	2	2	2	2	2	2	2	2	2	2
10	3	2	2	2	2	2	2	2	2	2

(Rises %)

If each transaction costs, say £4, then the area of most profitable investment will change.

In addition, the program may be modified so that a purchase on the first day is replaced by the *buyloop* approach of searching for a lower value. Consideration may also be given to the fact that buying or selling prices normally reach the public one day late via the newspapers, so that transactions take place one day after the criterion for buying or selling has been satisfied.

7

ADDITIONAL ALGOL

7.1 Introduction

In this chapter additional facilities of Algol, which are used in the later chapters of this book, are described.

7.2 Blocks and dynamic arrays

A compound statement, consisting of a sequence of statements enclosed within the statement brackets **begin** and **end**, becomes a block if it contains at least one declaration which must, according to the rules, immediately follow the word **begin**.
In many cases, a program can be constructed as a single block, with all the declarations at the beginning. It is, however, possible to have nested inner blocks. In this situation, the scope where any identifiers may be used is restricted to within the block in which they are declared.
The scope of a label is limited to the innermost block in which it appears and for Elliott 803 Algol must be declared in a switch declaration at the head of this block.
In the outermost block of a program the lower and upper bounds of array declarations must be constants. In an inner block, the bounds may be declared as the values of arithmetic expressions involving identifiers which have been declared and given values in an outer block. Such arrays with variable bounds are said to be dynamic arrays.
A further extension to the form of an array declaration is that identifiers of arrays of the same size may be listed together followed by the common bounds, thus

array $A, B, C\ [1:m, 1:n];$.

A typical use of a dynamic array is exemplified

48   PROGRAMMING BY CASE STUDIES

by the extension of the program in Section 3.2 to sort an array of a variable number of elements, not just the fixed number, 100.

It is assumed that the number of numbers to follow will be the first item of data.

Sort n numbers;
<u>begin</u>
    <u>integer</u> *n;*
    <u>read</u> *n;*
    <u>begin</u>
        <u>integer</u> *i,exchange;*
        <u>real</u> *store;*
        <u>array</u> *number* $[1:n]$;
        <u>switch</u> *s:=nextpass;*
        <u>for</u> *i:=1* <u>step</u> *1* <u>until</u> *n* <u>do</u> <u>read</u> *number* $[i]$;
nextpass: exchange:=0;
        <u>for</u> *i:=1* <u>step</u> *1* <u>until</u> *n-1* <u>do</u>
        <u>if</u> *number* $[i]$ > *number* $[i+1]$ <u>then</u>
        <u>begin</u>
            store:=number $[i+1]$;
            number $[i+1]$ *:=number* $[i]$;
            number $[i]$ *:=store;*
            exchange:=1
        end;
        <u>if</u> *exchange≠0* <u>then</u> <u>goto</u> *nextpass;*
        <u>for</u> *i:=1* <u>step</u> *1* <u>until</u> *n* <u>do</u> <u>print</u> *number* $[i]$
    end
end;

    The advantages of using dynamic arrays in a program are that the possibility of a considerable waste of storage area for the unrequired array elements is eliminated as well as the problem of finding suitable array bounds.

7.3 The <u>while</u> type of <u>for</u> list element

    The general form of the third type of <u>for</u> list element mentioned in Section 2.10 is

        arithmetic expression while *relationship.*

    The action of a <u>for</u> statement including this type of <u>for</u> list element is that the value of the arithmetic expression is repeatedly assigned to the controlled variable, the relationship being inspected after each assignment, and the statement following <u>do</u> executed provided that the relationship is true. If the relationship is not true, the <u>for</u> list element has been exhausted.

More than one type of <u>for</u> list element may be included in a <u>for</u> list, and it is frequently convenient to precede a <u>while</u>-element by the assignment of the value of a simple arithmetic expression to the controlled variable to initiate a process.

This kind of use of the <u>while</u>-element is illustrated by the following program to sum the series (for $\pi^4/96$)

$$\frac{1}{1^4} + \frac{1}{3^4} + \frac{1}{5^4} + \frac{1}{7^4} + \ldots$$

continuing until the terms are less than 10^{-8}.

Series summation;

<u>begin</u>
    <u>integer</u> *n;*
    <u>real</u> *sum, term;*

    sum:=0·0;

    <u>for</u> *n:=1,n+2* <u>while</u> *term* ≥ 10^{-8} <u>do</u>

    <u>begin</u>
        term:=n↑(-4);
        sum:=sum+term
    <u>end</u>;

    <u>print</u> *sum*
<u>end</u>;

7.4 Procedures

Algol provides a facility which allows a portion of program performing a standard routine to be inserted in a number of places in a program without writing it out in full each time but just once as a procedure declaration.

With a procedure is associated an identifier and its declaration consists of a heading including the identifier, possibly associated with a set of formal parameters, together with a body of Algol statements for performing the operation. When the procedure is called, the actual parameters are inserted in place of the corresponding formal parameters, and the procedure body is executed.

There are two ways of using procedures:
(1) as function designators which supply values through the procedure identifier for use in expressions,
(2) as procedure statements which may supply values through the parameters.

The standard functions provided by Algol are examples of function designators.

To provide a further function,

$$tan(AE)$$

for the tangent of an angle AE expressed in radians, its action must be defined by a procedure declaration.

All procedures must be declared in a block head. Elliott 803 Algol restricts procedure declarations to the end of a set of declarations.

The form of a procedure declaration is

(*type*) **procedure** *identifier*(FP,FP,...,FP);
value part
specification part
. . . . .
procedure body, ending with a semicolon.

An example of a procedure declaration for tan(AE) is

real procedure *tan(x)*;
value *x*; **real** *x*;
tan:=*sin(x)/cos(x)*;

It should be noted that a procedure which is to be used as a function designator must always have a type symbol, and one of the statements in the procedure body must assign a value to the procedure identifier.

The value part list of the procedure heading indicates whether a formal parameter is to be called by value or by name, the treatment being different when the procedure is entered. For call by value, the actual parameters are evaluated and assigned as initial values to the local formal parameters used in the procedure body. For call by name, the formal parameters are replaced by the actual parameters in the procedure body. To specify their uses the identifiers of the formal parameters must appear in a list preceded by an appropriate specifier such as **real**, **integer**, (**real**) **array** or **integer array**.

Procedures may also be used to replace sections

ADDITIONAL ALGOL   51

of program.
   An example of a declaration of a procedure for
reading data into elements of an array is

   <u>procedure</u> *readarray;*
   <u>for</u> *i:=1* <u>step</u> *1* <u>until</u> *n* <u>do</u> <u>read</u> *A*[*i*];.

After such a declaration the 'procedure call' statement
                  readarray;
could replace the <u>for</u> statement in a program and would
read a number of data values corresponding to the
current value of the variable with identifier *n* into
the elements of the array with identifier *A*, both *n*
and *A*, as well as *i*, being declared in the main program.
   As the identifier *i* is unassigned outside the <u>for</u>
statement it may be considered local to the procedure
and could usefully be declared at the head of a block
within the procedure body, in which case the identifier *i* could be used for some other purpose in the main
program.
   It might also prove useful to be able to read a
variable number of data values into arrays with identifiers other than *A*. To achieve this facility the
identifiers *n* and *A* should be specified as formal
parameters.
   Thus a modified version of the procedure declaration might be

   <u>procedure</u> *readarray(A,n);*
   <u>value</u> *n;* <u>integer</u> *n;* <u>array</u> *A;*
   <u>begin</u>
         <u>integer</u> *i;*
         <u>for</u> *i:=1* <u>step</u> *1* <u>until</u> *n* <u>do</u> <u>read</u> *A*[*i*]
   <u>end</u>;

   It should be noted that in order to insert values
in the actual array appearing as a parameter in the
statement calling the procedure, the corresponding
formal parameter, array *A*, must be called by name.
   Familiarity with the use of procedures enables
advantage to be taken of the large number of published
Algol procedures for performing standard types of
computation.

7.5 <u>Comment facilities</u>

   Explanatory comments, for the benefit of a human

reader only, may be included in an Algol program in
statements of the form:

 comment *text not containing a semicolon;*

An example occurs in Section 11.4.

8
SIMPLE SIMULATION: SNAKES AND LADDERS

8.1 The problem

Most people have played games of snakes and ladders in their lives; most when they were very young, or when they were entertaining the young. It is a game of chance, a game where the throw of a die dominates the course of the game.

Quite clearly it is possible at any stage to work out the chances of hitting a snake or a ladder at any one time for any one throw, but for more than about 3 throws it becomes very difficult. Consequently it would be difficult to compare two different arrangements by theoretical means. The only real way is to play each game a few hundred times to see how each game fares - and who, of a mature age, would want to play snakes and ladders a few hundred times?

The problem therefore resolves itself into programming a computer to play a game of snakes and ladders. It must be done in such a way that one can compare two or more arrangements of snakes and ladders over a period of a hundred or more games.

8.2 The simulation of a die

Clearly, if one is to make a computer play snakes and ladders, it is necessary to be able to make the computer, in effect, throw a die. Throwing a die is to choose a number between 1 and 6 so that each of the numbers 1, 2, 3, 4, 5 and 6 can occur at any time with equal probability.

Thus in order to throw a die, the computer generates a random number. This is a well-known computer technique which may be achieved in a variety of ways by programming.

All of the programming techniques used (whenever the computer does not use its own built-in random number generator) have one facet in common. That is, whenever the random number generator procedure is used,

it can always start with the same value. This is a
great advantage when testing programs on the computer,
and its disadvantages are minimised since the sequence
of random numbers generated will continue each time
the procedure is used.

It will therefore be assumed that a suitable random number generator procedure is available which
will generate integers in the range a to b inclusive
by referring to

$$random(a,b).$$

For simplicity, the procedure will be assumed to
be of the most elementary form in which a digit 0-9
is read from a set of random digits in a data stream.
As these digits are read into the computer they must
be tested to see if they lie in the appropriate range;
if not they are rejected and others considered in
their places.

```
          integer procedure random(a,b);
          value a,b; integer a,b;
          begin
                    integer digit;
                    switch s:=outofrange;
outofrange: read digit;
                    if digit<a then goto outofrange;
                    if digit>b then goto outofrange;
                    random:=digit
          end;
```

8.3 The approach to the problem

Essentially, the game of snakes and ladders is
played with a counter moving over 100 squares. It is,
therefore, necessary to keep a record of the square
which the counter occupies at any one time.

The throw is made, the counter moved and then
transferred up a ladder or down a snake if appropriate. Thus after the counter is moved to say, square
46 it would appear necessary to go through a list of
ladders to see if one starts on square 46, or to see
if a snake starts on square 46.

If this technique is adopted, then, seeing that
there are usually about 10 each of ladders and snakes,
a search will have to be made of the 20 jump movements to find if one exists. In 4 out of 5 times,
this search will provide the fact that there is no
appropriate jump. This is quite clearly going to be

SIMPLE SIMULATION: SNAKES AND LADDERS   55

wasteful of computer time, so that it is appropriate
to find a shorter method.
   Suppose now we consider an array *board* of 100
locations which are numbered from *board*[1] to *board*[100].
Let the contents of each location be held to be the
number of the square after the jump. Thus, if there
is a ladder starting on square 46 running to square
84, then the content of *board*[46] would be 84. If
square 53 had a snake running to square 13, the content of *board*[53] would be 13, but if square 68 had
neither snake nor ladder, then *board*[68] would contain 68.
   If the technique adopted is that variable *square*
denotes the position of the counter after the throw,
then the effect of the snake or ladder or neither is
very simply effected by the statement

$$square := board\,[square];$$

```
100 99 98 97 96 95 94 93 92 91     100 61 98 56 96 95 94 93 92 91
 81 82 83 84 85 86 87 88 89 90      81 82 83 84 85 86 87 93 89 48
 80 79 78 77 76 75 74 73 72 71      80 19 78 77 76 75 74 73 72 71
 61 62 63 64 65 66 67 68 69 70      61 62 63 64 87 66 67 68 69 70
 60 59 58 57 56 55 54 53 52 51      40 59 58 82 56 55 54 74 52 51
 41 42 43 44 45 46 47 48 49 50      41 42 43 15 66 46 47 48 49 28
 40 39 38 37 36 35 34 33 32 31      40 39 38 37 36 35 34 33 72 31
 21 22 23 24 25 26 27 28 29 30      62 22 23 24 25  8 27 28 29 30
 20 19 18 17 16 15 14 13 12 11      20 19 18 17 37 15 49 13 12 11
  1  2  3  4  5  6  7  8  9 10       1  2  3 38  5  6  7  8  9 10
```

    The actual board   *The program array board*
                                             which corresponds to the
                                             actual board used (left)

Figure 8/1 - Snakes and Ladders Board A

   All that has then to be ensured is that the content of the array is arranged correctly when the
snakes and ladders of each game are defined. The
array for a specific set of snakes and ladders is
given in Figure 8/1.

8.4 The details of the problem

   This approach means that the program must generate an array in which the content of each element is
the same as the suffix of the array *board*.
   If the data are in the form of the starting point

and finishing point represented by a pair of integers, then any number of these may be fed in with, say, a zero after the last pair of numbers.

Typical sets of data are shown in Figure 8/2.

In the actual play, it is not usual to throw a 'six' to start; in this case the starting position of the counter is zero. Any throw made may be added on, with the jump effected after the throw.

Set A (as in Figure 8/1)		Set B	
Snakes	Ladders	Snakes	Ladders
26 - 8	4 - 38	26 - 8	14 - 49
46 - 15	14 - 49	50 - 28	21 - 62
50 - 28	16 - 37	67 - 35	45 - 66
60 - 40	21 - 62	90 - 48	65 - 87
67 - 35	32 - 72	99 - 61	88 - 93
79 - 19	45 - 66		
90 - 48	53 - 74		
97 - 56	65 - 87		
99 - 61	57 - 82		
	88 - 93		

Figure 8/2 - Typical Sets of Data

When the counter has reached square 94 or over, then the game is near the end, and any throw may result in 100 being reached or exceeded. The usual limitation is that the counter must land exactly on square 100. If 100 is exceeded the throw is not permitted, and must be withdrawn. It is not possible, however, to subtract a throw unless it has been recorded, for calling *random(1,6)* again will merely produce another throw, which may of course be different.

At this stage, for the basic problem, the number of throws can be printed out, together with the mean number of throws for the 100 games.

SIMPLE SIMULATION: SNAKES AND LADDERS 57

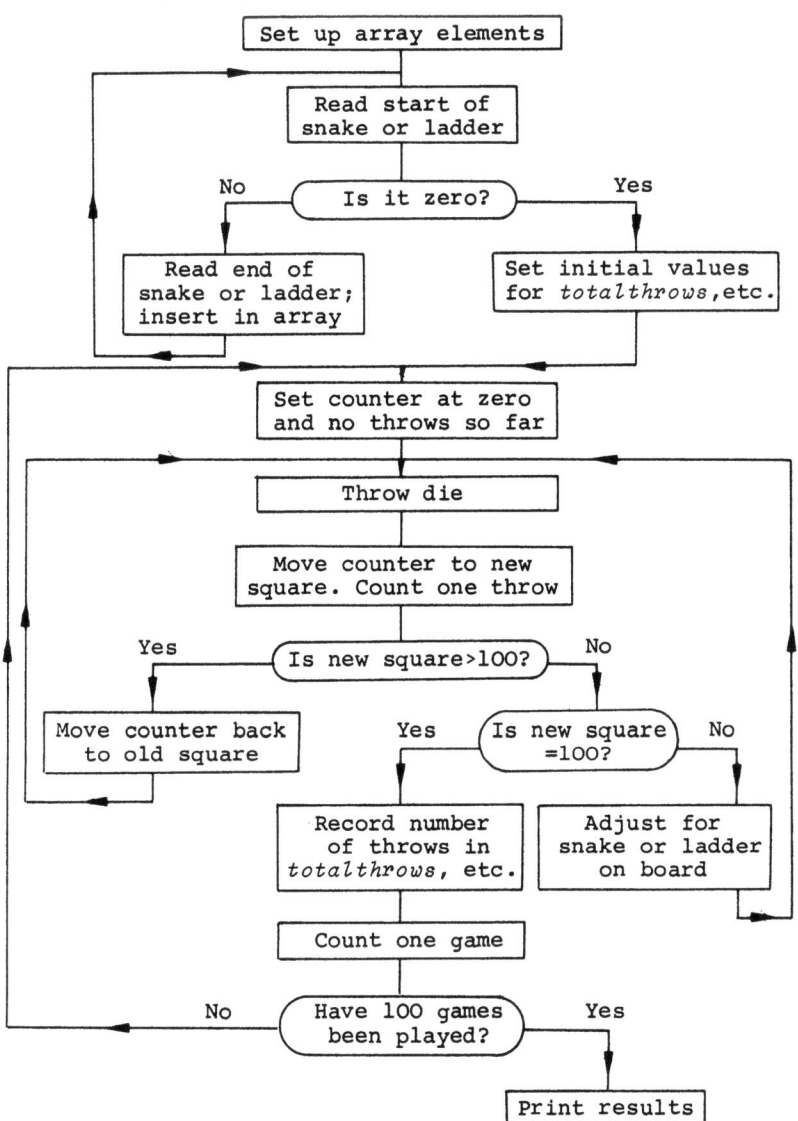

8.5 The program

```
Snakes and Ladders;
begin
      integer i,square,start,finish,throws,totalthrows,
              maxthrows,minthrows,die;
      real meanthrows;
      integer array board[1:100];
      switch s:=next,again,home;
      integer procedure random(a,b);
      value a,b; integer a,b;
      begin
            integer digit;
            switch s:=outofrange;
outofrange: read digit;
            if digit<a then goto outofrange;
            if digit>b then goto outofrange;
            random:=digit
      end;
      for i:=1 step 1 until 100 do board[i]:=i;
next: read start;
      if start≠0 then
      begin read finish;
            board[start]:=finish;
            goto next
      end;
      maxthrows:=totalthrows:=0;
      minthrows:=1000;
      for i:=1 step 1 until 100 do
      begin
            throws:=square:=0;
again:      die:=random(1,6);
            square:=square+die;
            throws:=throws+1;
            if square>100 then square:=square-die
            else
            if square=100 then goto home;
            square:=board[square];
            goto again;
home:       totalthrows:=totalthrows+throws;
            if maxthrows<throws then maxthrows:=throws;
            if minthrows>throws then minthrows:=throws
      end;
      meanthrows:=totalthrows/100·0;
      print maxthrows,meanthrows,minthrows
end;
```

SIMPLE SIMULATION: SNAKES AND LADDERS   59

8.6 The results

The two games shown in Figure 8/2 were simulated by a computer in this way, giving the following results. For comparison, a game with no snakes and ladders at all was also played 100 times.

	Number of throws in 100 games		
	Maximum	Mean	Minimum
Game A	154	40·70	12
Game B	83	33·34	10
Game with no snakes and ladders	74	43·30	23

It is thus seen that the introduction of snakes and ladders tends to increase the range of the number of throws required to complete the game, but seems to have little overall effect on the mean.

8.7 Comments on the program

There are variations on the play of the game.

In some methods of play it is necessary to throw a six before one is able to start the game at square 1.

Another of the variations occurs when the counter is nearing the final square. If a throw is made which takes the counter effectively beyond the 100 mark, the rules may call for the surplus of the throw to act in reflection, resulting in the counter being moved backwards opening the way for further snake pitfalls.

These and other variations can easily be fitted in to the program described.

It is also possible to consider other methods of generating the random throws of a die. When this is done, the new method is written as a procedure with the same specification, and merely replaces the previous procedure in the program.

Methods of generating random numbers tend to be related to a specific computer, but the general principles used are similar. Most computer units have procedures available for this type of generation.

The program may also be extended to calculate not only the means and ranges of the throws required, but also the standard deviation, for each sample. The modification required is slight, and the additional calculation may be very simply incorporated.

9

CALIBRATION OF A DEPTH GAUGE
USE OF APPROXIMATION

9.1 The problem

For the purpose of calibrating a depth gauge for a specially shaped tank, it is required to relate the depth to equal increments of the volume of liquid contained in the tank.

The type of tank we shall consider here is typical of that used in distillation works, and comprises a horizontal cylinder with dished ends consisting of spherical domes. The cross-section of such a tank is shown in Figure 9/1.

Figure 9/1 - Cross-section of horizontally cylindrical tank with spherical dished ends

9.2 Simplified approach : Method

In the initial assessment of the problem, let us ignore the dished ends, so that we shall look first of all at a horizontally cylindrical tank with flat ends.

From inspection of a circular cross-section of a tank, of radius r, as shown in Figure 9/2, it is clear that, if the liquid in the tank has a maximum depth h, for h less than the radius r, the area of the segment filled with liquid can be found by subtracting the area of the triangle OAB from the area of the sector OAB.

CALIBRATION OF A DEPTH GAUGE   61

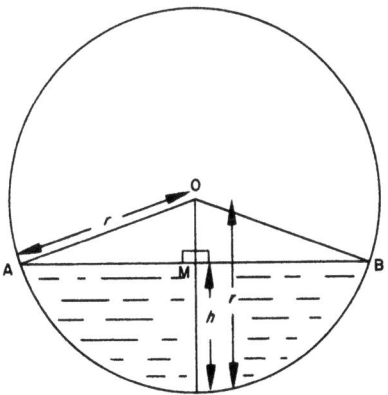

Figure 9/2 - Circular cross-section of tank

To find these areas we require the length AB and the angle AOB. Applying Pythagoras' theorem to the right-andled triangle OAM, where M is the midpoint of the chord AB we get

$$AM^2 = OA^2 - OM^2$$
$$= r^2 - (r - h)^2$$
$$= h(2r - h).$$

Thus $AB = 2AM = 2\sqrt{h(2r - h)}$,

and $A\hat{O}B = 2A\hat{O}M = 2\tan^{-1}\left(\frac{AM}{OM}\right) = 2\tan^{-1}\left(\frac{\sqrt{h(2r - h)}}{r - h}\right)$.

The areas of the triangle and sector OAB are now readily found to be

$$(r - h)\sqrt{h(2r - h)}$$

and $r^2 \tan^{-1}\left(\frac{\sqrt{h(2r - h)}}{r - h}\right)$ respectively.

Hence, if l is the length of the tank, the volume V of the liquid content of maximum depth h, less than the radius r of the cylinder, is given by

$$V = \left(r^2\tan^{-1}\left(\frac{\sqrt{h(2r - h)}}{r - h}\right) - (r - h)\sqrt{h(2r - h)}\right)l.$$

It is obvious from the complexity of this formula that it would not be an easy task to find the depth h for a specified volume V, whereas it is relatively simple to calculate V given h, r and l.

This fact straightaway suggests a method of approach for the solution of our problem. Bearing in mind the speed at which a computer performs arithmetic, it is feasible to calculate the volume for a succession of values of the depth using sufficiently small increments until a required calibration value of the volume is achieved, with, of course, a known value of the corresponding depth.

9.3 Simplified approach : application

The formula derived in Section 9.2 for the area of a segment, of depth h, of a circle of radius r, for h less than r, could usefully be calculated in a program by means of a function designator of type <u>real</u> with the parameters r and h, say $segarea(r,h)$.

The volume of liquid, with greatest depth h, in a horizontal cylinder of radius r and length l would then be

$l \times segarea(r,h)$ for $h < r$,

$l \times \frac{1}{2} \pi r^2$ for $h = r$,

$l \times (\pi r^2 - segarea(r, 2r-h))$ for $r < h < 2r$,

$l \times \pi r^2$ for $h = 2r$.

The repetitive calculation involved in the method of solution proposed in 9.2 is elegantly achieved in an Algol program by the use of a <u>for</u> statement with a <u>while</u>-element, although the same effect may be obtained using <u>if</u> and <u>goto</u> statements.

A further point about the method, which should be considered before programming is started, is that it will be necessary to test for the tank becoming full, in order to avoid either of the situations with the depth of the liquid exceeding the diameter of the cylinder or the volume calibrations exceeding the capacity of the tank.

Finally, it must be decided in which units, items, forming part of the input and output data, should be measured. The program in Section 9.4 assumes that the length and radius of the cylinder and the depth increment will be supplied in inches and the calibration interval in gallons. The relationship between the two

CALIBRATION OF A DEPTH GAUGE

types of measure is that 1 cubic foot (1728 cubic inches) is equivalent to 6·24 imperial gallons.
A flow diagram is given in Figure 9/3.

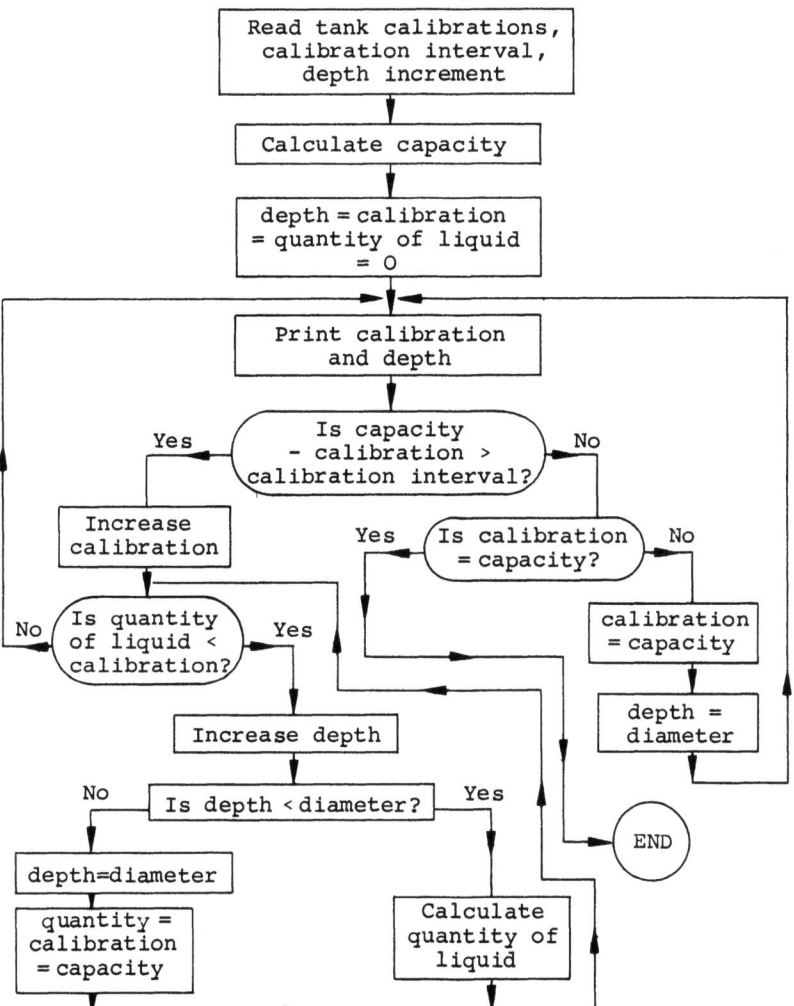

Figure 9/3 - Flow diagram for calibrating a depth gauge for a tank

9.4 Program for tank with flat ends

Calibration of depth gauge for tank with flat ends;
```
begin
      real l,r,h,dh,capacity,calibration,
      quantity,interval,diff,z,pi,A;
      switch s:=loop,exit;
      real procedure segarea(r,h);
      value r,h; real r,h;
      begin
            real x,y;
            x:=r-h;
            y:=sqrt(h×(r+x));
            segarea:=r×r×arctan(y/x)-x×y
      end;
      pi:=3·14159 2654;
      read l,r,interval,dh;
      capacity:=0·00361×pi×r×r×l;
      comment conversion factor between units=0·00361;
      h:=calibration:=quantity:=0·0;
loop:print calibration,h;
      diff:=capacity-calibration;
      if diff>interval then
      calibration:=calibration+interval
      else if abs(diff)<$10^{-4}$ then goto exit else
      begin
            calibration:=capacity;
            h:=r+r;
            goto loop
      end;
      for z:=h+dh while quantity<calibration do
      begin
            h:=z;
            if r+r-h$\geq 10^{-4}$ then
            begin
                  if h<r then A:=segarea(r,h) else
                  begin
                        A:=0·5×pi×r×r;
                        if h>r then A:=A+A-segarea(r,r+r-h)
                  end;
                  quantity:=0·00361×A×l
            end else
            begin
                  h:=r+r;
                  quantity:=calibration:=capacity
            end
      end;
      goto loop;
exit:
end;
```

9.5 Results for tank with flat ends

For data: length 120 length 120 inches
radius 36 inches
calibration interval 100 gallons
depth increment ·05 inches

Calibration in gallons	Depth in inches
0	·00000000
100	7·6500007
200	12·300002
300	16·350002
400	20·049999
500	23·499996
600	26·899992
700	30·149989
800	33·399986
900	36·599983
1000	39·799983
1100	43·049977
1200	46·349974
1300	49·749971
1400	53·299967
1500	57·099964
1600	61·349965
1700	66·349965
1764·3184	72·000000

9.6 Extension of method for dished ends

We now return to the original problem and see how we may extend the method used for the simplified approach to cater for a horizontally cylindrical tank with spherical dished ends.

By consulting a reference book of geometrical formulae, it can be found that the volume of a spherical cap of height k is

$$\frac{\pi k^2}{3} (3r_s - k)$$

where r_s is the radius of the sphere.

To find the radius of the sphere for the dished ends we consider the cross-section of a spherical cap shown in Figure 9/4.

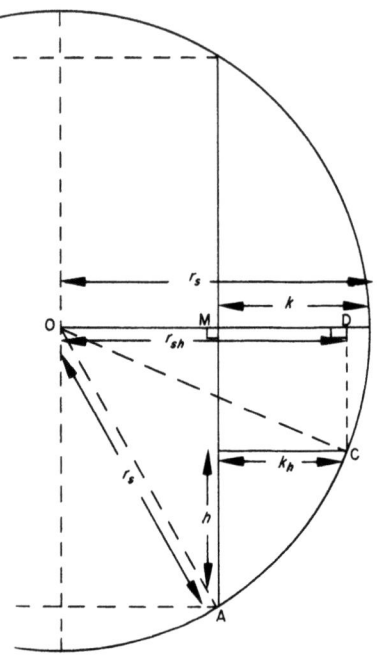

Figure 9/4 - Vertical cross-section of spherical dished end

If O is the centre of the sphere, by applying Pythagoras' theorem, firstly to the triangle, OAM, we have
$$r_s^2 = (r_s - k)^2 + r^2,$$
from which we obtain
$$s = \frac{1}{2}\left(\frac{r^2}{k} + k\right),$$
and secondly, to the triangle OCD, we have
$$OD^2 = OC^2 - CD^2$$
or
$$r_{sh} = \sqrt{r_s^2 - (r - h)^2}$$
= radius of the circular horizontal cross-section segment of the spherical cap.

CALIBRATION OF A DEPTH GAUGE

It is clear from the diagram that the depth of this segment,

$$k_h = r_{sh} - r_s + k.$$

Now suppose we increase the depth h of the liquid content by a small amount dh, the increase in the volume of the liquid in a spherical cap is approximately equal to dh times the area of the horizontal cross-sectional segment of the cap at a depth $h + \frac{1}{2}dh$. See Figure 9/5.

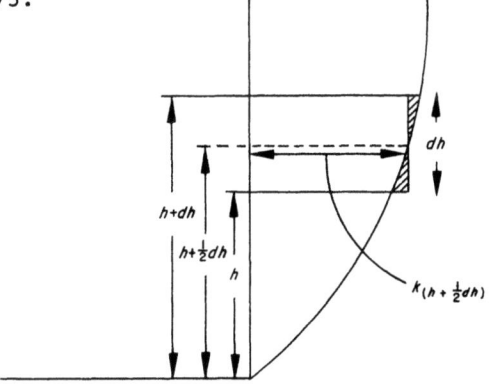

Figure 9/5

Thus by summing the volume increments for sufficiently small increments of depth dh we can obtain good approximations to the volume of liquid in a spherical cap as we increase the depth h.

9.7 Extension of program for dished ends

Since we already have a procedure for calculating the area of a segment of a circle, only a small amount of extra programming is required to incorporate the spherical dished ends.

A running total of the volume increments for the spherical caps must be kept and the current total added into the volume of the liquid content of the cylindrical part of the tank for each increment in the depth.

The flow diagram given in Figure 9/3 for the program in 9.4 is still applicable for the extended program.

9.8 The program
Calibration of depth gauge for tank with spherical dished ends;

```
begin real l,r,h,dh,capacity,calibration,quantity,
    interval,diff,z,pi,A,k,rs,rsh,kh,volsh;
    switch s:=loop,exit;
    real procedure segarea(r,h);
    value r,h; real r,h;
    begin real x,y;
        x:=r-h; y:=sqrt(h×(r+x));
        segarea:=r×r×arctan(y/x)-x×y
    end;
    pi:=3·14159265 4;
    read l,r,k,interval,dh;
    rs:=0·5×(r×r/k+k);
    capacity:=0·00361×pi×(r×r×l+2·0×k×k×(rs-k/3·0));
    comment conversion factor between units:=0·00361;
    h:=calibration:=quantity:=volsh:=0·0;
loop:print calibration,h;
    diff:=capacity-calibration;
    if diff>interval then
    calibration:=calibration+interval
    else if abs(diff)<10-4 then goto exit else
    begin
        calibration:=capacity; h:=r+r;
        goto loop
    end;
    for z:=h+dh while quantity<calibration do
    begin
        h:=z;
        if r+r-h⩾10-4 then
        begin
            rsh:=sqrt(rs×rs-(r-h+0·5×dh)↑2);
            kh:=rsh-rs+k;
            volsh:=volsh+dh×segarea(rsh,kh);
            if h<r then A:=segarea(r,h) else
            begin
                A:=0·5×pi×r×r;
                if h>r then A:=A+A-segarea(r,r+r-h)
            end;
            quantity:=0·00361×(a×l+volsh+volsh)
        end else
        begin
            h:=r+r; quantity:=calibration+capacity
        end
    end;
    goto loop;
exit:
end;
```

CALIBRATION OF A DEPTH GAUGE

9.9 Results for tank with spherical dished ends

Results for data concerning a tank with basic dimensions of
  length = 120 inches
  radius = 36 inches
  calibration interval = 100 gallons
are given below.

(1) A tank with very shallow dished ends, that is, the height of the spherical dome is taken as ·1 inches, is compared with a similar tank with flat ends. For convenience the results of 9.5 are repeated here.
In both cases the depth increment used in the calculation was the same at ·05 inches.

Calibration in gallons	Tank with dished ends Depth in inches	Tank with flat ends Depth in inches
0	·00000000	·00000000
100	7·6500007	7·6500007
200	12·300002	12·300002
300	16·350002	16·350002
400	19·999999	20·049999
500	23·499996	23·499996
600	26·849992	26·899992
700	30·149989	30·149989
800	33·349986	33·399986
900	36·549983	36·599983
1000	39·799980	39·799983
1100	42·999977	43·049977
1200	46·299974	46·349974
1300	49·699971	49·749971
1400	53·249967	53·299967
1500	57·049963	57·099964
1600	61·249960	61·349965
1700	66·299965	66·349965
1765·7928	72·000000	
1764·3184		72·000000

(2) A tank with a significant size in the dished ends, that is, a height of the spherical dome of 6 inches, was evaluated using two different depth increments: ·05 inches and ·01 inches. For convenience the results are listed side by side.

Calibration in gallons	Increment of ·05 inches Depth in inches	Increment of ·01 inches Depth in inches
0	·00000000	·00000000
100	7·6000007	7·5599975
200	12·100002	12·089993
300	16·000003	15·979989
400	19·549999	19·519986
500	22·899996	22·859983
600	26·049993	26·049980
700	29·149990	29·149977
800	32·199987	32·189974
900	35·199984	35·199971
1000	38·249982	38·209968
1100	41·249979	41·229965
1200	44·299976	44·299962
1300	47·449976	47·439959
1400	50·699970	50·689956
1500	54·149966	54·109953
1600	57·799963	57·789949
1700	61·949959	61·919946
1800	67·099968	67·060013
1853·3555	72·000000	72·000000

9.10 Remarks on the results

It is worth-while noticing the program check provided by the good correspondence between the results for a flat-ended tank in 9.5 and the first set of results in 9.9 for a tank with insignificantly dished ends. The decrease in the depth for the latter tank at a particular calibration value is never more than ·05 inches.

The two sets of results achieved for the tank with the dome of height 6 inches show the difference achieved in using two different increment levels of depth.

The time taken for the computer run was, as might be expected, 5 times as long for the increment of ·01 inches as it was for the increment of ·05 inches: 75 minutes compared with 15 minutes.

Examination of the two sets of results shows that use of a larger interval does not introduce any overall cumulative error, but only the inevitable loss of precision in the depth calculation. Hence it would be extremely difficult to justify the increase in computer time required for the computation in order to achieve the increased accuracy.

The rounding errors seen in the depths for all four sets of results suggest an improvement in the method employed to increase the depth h, along the lines of
$$h:=n \times dh;$$
$$n:=n+1;$$
where n is **integer**.

9.11 Units

This example has been computed in gallons and inches; it is a simple matter to change the programs to operate in metric or any other units.

10

JOB PLANNING
A PROBLEM IN OPTIMIZATION

10.1 The problem

The problem in this case is to find an optimum arrangement of a given set of data.

The data set refers to a group of 8 projects in a factory concerning certain improvements which have to be made. These projects are of such a nature that, once started, they must be followed through to completion; but it does not matter which is started first provided that all 8 are completed within a period of 32 weeks.

The estimated cost of these improvements are given, and the starting times must be arranged as that the total weekly cost is as near as possible constant.

The estimated costs are as follows:

Project	Costs in £, starting at first week
1	50 50 50 100 100 100 150 150 200 200 100 100 100 100
2	80 80 80 80 80 150 150 150 150 150 200 200 200 300 300 300 100 100 100 50
3	40 40 50 50 60 60 70 70 80 80 90 90 100 100 110 150 150 150 50 50
4	90 90 90 150 200 100 200 200 100 100
5	100 100 110 110 160 160 160 160 180 180 100 50
6	100 120 200 220 220 200 180 80
7	100 100 200 200 150 350 350 300 200 100
8	50 60 70 80 90 100 200 200 90 80 70

10.2 The method

An obvious method is to try all possible arrange-

72

JOB PLANNING: A PROBLEM IN OPTIMIZATION 73

ments of the data to see which gives us the best answer. A quick investigation shows that Project 1 could start in weeks 1 to 19, i.e. 19 possible ways. Project 2 could start in 13 ways, and so on.

If each of the combinations of starting times is tried then there is a total of

$$19 \times 13 \times 13 \times 23 \times 21 \times 25 \times 23 \times 22$$

or about 10^{10} ways. If each arrangement takes only 1 second to check, the whole computation will take no less than about 300,000 hours - and this is quite clearly unacceptable and unrealistic for finding the answer to this problem.

A shorter method must be found. A possible new approach is by (random) 'trial and error'; a phrase which the evolutionist Huxley suggested replacing by 'fumbling and success'.

Suppose a trial arrangement is taken with the 8 projects starting at random within the 32 weeks, ensuring that they all finish before the end of the last week (Figure 10/1). Now by considering the last 7 to be fixed, the starting date of the first one is moved into all possible arrangements, and the one which gives the best result is then picked.

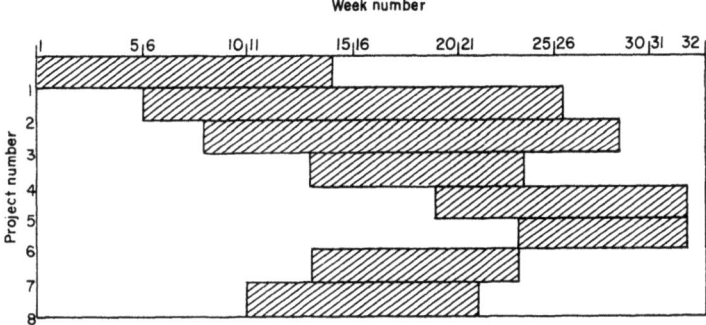

Figure 10/1 - Trial Arrangement of Projects

Now the first and the last 6 projects are fixed, and the second project is varied to give the starting date of the best result. The process is repeated for the remainder of the projects.

Thus to go through the 8 projects will take

19 + 13 + 13 + 23 + 21 + 25 + 23 + 22

considerations of arrangements, that is 159 arrangements. Of course, it must be remembered that even when the whole eight have been fixed, it may be possible to start again at the first and improve it, because the arrangement of the last 7 has been altered since the previous time.

It is possible to vary this approach again, because if one looks reasonably closely at the data, the expenditure in general reaches a peak for each project in the middle. Thus, if the starting date of a project is moved, the arrangement is likely to get better and better up to a certain point, and then start getting worse again. If this point can be detected, there is little value in checking further.

The second project can be checked in a similar way, and so on.

This approach compared with the previous one will reduce the number of arrangements to be considered by a further factor of about 3, since it is easy to determine the direction in which the project has to be moved, and to find out when the move has gone far enough.

This is the method adopted for the calculation.

10.3 The criterion for 'optimum arrangement'

The initial problem stated that the total cost must be as nearly as possible constant over the period of 32 weeks. It is quite clearly impossible to get absolute constancy, since all projects build up to a peak.

Hence, there must be a criterion of 'best fit' before the problem can be seriously tackled. There are several approaches, but for the purpose of this problem, the most obvious method is that of 'least squares'.

This will be familiar to anyone with a knowledge of statistics, but the principle is simple and will be readily appreciated by others.

Firstly, the total cost of all the projects is divided by 32 to give an idealised value of weekly cost. Then the difference between this idealised value and the computed value for each week is squared, and the total of these squared values is added for all 32 weeks. This total provides a convenient index of how far the particular scheme departs from the ideal.

It will be clear that this technique will minimise

the large differences, since when squared these become much larger still, but the smaller differences which make only small contributions to the total will be less affected.

10.4 The application of the method

Data storage   The first consideration of this program must be to allocate conveniently the storage of the data. This is achieved by an array, a, of 32×8 storage locations which hold the actual costs. This layout is illustrated in Figure 10/1 which shows also two one-dimensional arrays called *weekcost*, where the 32 totals of weekly expenditure are held, and *start* whose 8 elements contain the starting-week numbers of each project.

Procedures   The method requires 3 particular techniques more than once. In order to reduce the length of the program, these are written as separate procedures, and then called for by the procedure name. These procedures are called *deviationcost*, *laterproject* and *earlierproject*, and are declared at the beginning of the program.

Deviationcost is the first of these procedures. The procedure uses an additional integer variable *count* which occurs nowhere in the main program. The method is to deal with the array week by week, and within each week, the values of the eight projects are added into the corresponding *weekcost* array element. When these eight have been accumulated then the square of the differences between that accumulated total and the weekly meancost is calculated and added into the store called *ssdev* (standing for sums of squares of deviations). When all 32 weeks have been dealt with in this way, *ssdev* contains the overall sums of squares of deviations. Thus the procedure *deviationcost* will put a measure on the overall array situation at any one time.

The procedure *laterproject* will take any project and move all the estimated costs later by one week. Notice that in order to do this, they have to be moved from week 31 to week 32, then week 30 to 31 and so on - ensuring that after the last move the value for week 1 is zero.

The procedure *earlierproject* works in a similar manner but, of course, in the reverse direction.

The main program   The complete flow diagram for the calculation is given in Figure 10/2.

The program now divides itself naturally into a familiar pattern: input, calculation and output.

Input   The input part of the program assumes at the same time a definition of the layout of the data. In this case the data is assumed to be available as a series of numbers which are in eight blocks, each containing

> an estimated starting week,
> the total number of weeks involved, and
> the estimated cost for each week.

Assuming this definition, every element in the array a is made equal to zero; the budget total made zero and the data read in project by project. The first two values are read into i,j and then these two values control all the remaining information to be read in. As each estimated value is read, it is also added to the budget total.

When all 8 projects have been treated in this way then the budget total is divided by 32 to give *meancost*, the ideal expenditure every week, and this value is printed out.

Calculation   At this stage it is possible to start the calculation proper, and the first step is to work out the value of *ssdev* which gives a minimum value for later comparison, and this value is, therefore, copied into variable *mincost*. The project counter is started with a value of 1.

If it is possible to move the project to start later (which means that week 32 of that project is zero), then it is started later by one week. A new value of *ssdev* is calculated and this is then compared with the value in variable *mincost*. If *ssdev* is greater than *mincost* then no improvement has been achieved, and, therefore, the project is moved earlier by one week in order to recover the previous position, and the second half of the calculation is attempted. If *ssdev* is less than *mincost* then an improvement has been achieved, and, therefore, the value of *ssdev* is entered as the new *mincost* value. The starting week for that project is increased by 1 and the values relating to that move printed out. The whole process of trying to start a week later is then tried again by taking the next statement in sequence to be the one

JOB PLANNING: A PROBLEM IN OPTIMIZATION 77

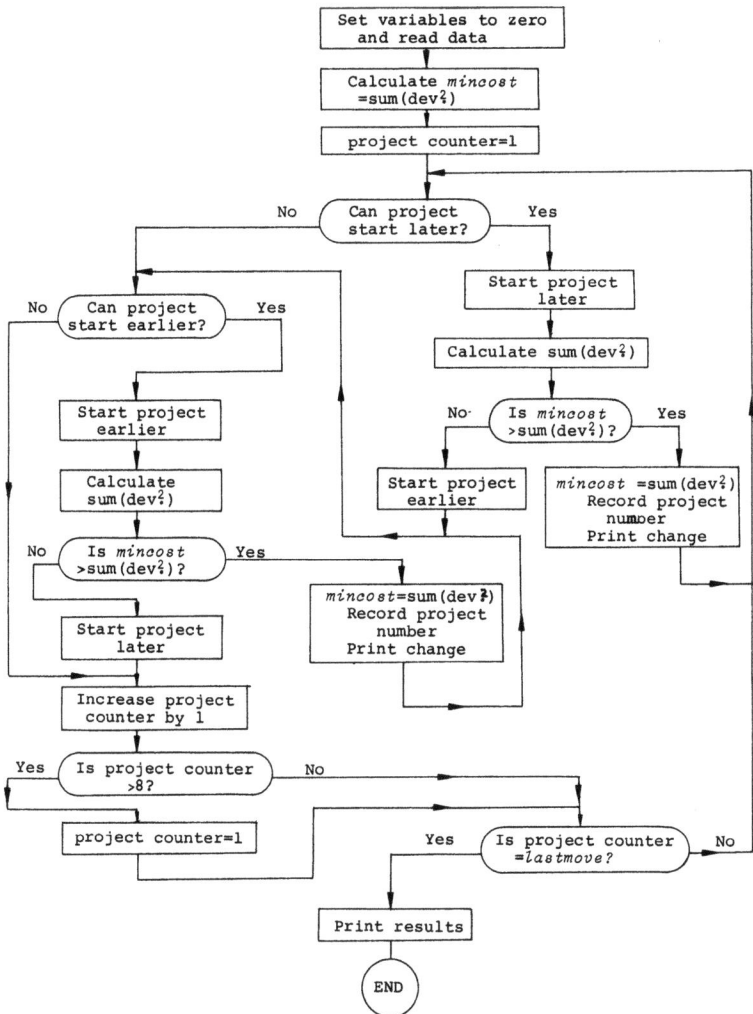

Figure 10/2 - Flow Diagram

preceded by the label *latemove*. Eventually, when the best situation has been reached, the statement following the label *earlymove* will be reached.

The second half of the calculation is similar to the first half, with the exception that it tries to move the project under consideration earlier rather than later, and, consequently, becomes virtually a mirror image of the first half.

When the second half has been completed, the project is assumed to be in the optimum position in relation to all the others, and the next project must be considered. This is done by adding 1 to the project counter, but ensuring that, if it has exceeded 9, it returns to 1.

The whole process is thus cyclic, and the only thing left to determine is when there is no further adjustment to be made for improvement. If the criterion is adopted that when a full cycle of attempts to improve have in fact resulted in no adjustments, then we have an easy answer.

When each move for improvement is accepted, this fact is recorded in an indicator *lastmove* which merely records the number of the project under consideration. Then when the project counter has been increased by 1 at the end of the optimization for each project, it is compared with *lastmove*. If they are the same, a complete cycle of improvements must have been attempted and produced nothing. This is then the end of the calculation.

<u>Output</u> The first stage of the output is to call up the procedure *deviationcost* which will recalculate the *weekcost* values since they will, in general, be incorrect as they are now arranged.

The *weekcost* totals are included in the printed output at the most appropriate point, which is when all the contributions from each project for that week have been printed out.

JOB PLANNING: A PROBLEM IN OPTIMIZATION

10.5 The program

```
Optimization problem;
begin
    real ssdev,mincost,meancost,budget;
    integer project,week,i,j,lastmove;
    array a[1:8, 1:32],weekcost[1:32];
    integer array start[1:8];
    switch s:=latemove,earlymove;
    procedure deviationcost;
    begin
        integer count;
        ssdev:=0·0;
        for week:=1 step 1 until 32 do
        begin
            weekcost[week]:=0·0;
            for count:=1 step 1 until 8 do
            weekcost[week]:=weekcost[week]
                +a[count,week];
            ssdev:=ssdev+(weekcost[week]-meancost)↑2
        end
    end;
    procedure laterproject;
    begin
        for week:=31 step -1 until 1 do
        a[project,week+1]:=a[project,week];
        a[project,1]:=0·0
    end;
    procedure earlierproject;
    begin
        for week:=1 step 1 until 31 do
        a[project,week]:=a[project,week+1];
        a[project,32]:=0·0
    end;
    for project:=1 step 1 until 8 do
    for week:=1 step 1 until 32 do
    a[project,week]:=0·0;
    budget:=0·0;
    for project:=1 step 1 until 8 do
    begin
        read i,j;
        start[project]:=i;
        for week:=i step 1 until i+j-1 do
        begin
            read a[project,week];
            budget:=budget+a[project,week]
        end
    end;
```

```
        meancost:=budget/32·0;
        print meancost;
        deviationcost;
        mincost:=ssdev;
        project:=1;
latemove: if a[project,32]=0·0 then
        begin
                laterproject;
                deviationcost;
                if mincost>ssdev then
                begin
                        mincost:=ssdev;
                        start[project]:=start[project]+1;
                        print project,mincost,start[project];
                        lastmove:=project;
                        goto latemove
                end;
                earlierproject
        end;
earlymove: if a[project,1]=0·0 then
        begin
                earlierproject;
                deviationcost;
                if mincost>ssdev then
                begin
                        mincost:=ssdev;
                        start[project]:=start[project]-1;
                        print project,mincost,start[project];
                        lastmove:=project;
                        goto earlymove
                end;
                laterproject
        end;
        project:=project+1;
        if project>8 then
        project:=1;
        if lastmove≠project then
        goto latemove;
        deviationcost;
        for week:=1 step 1 until 32 do
        begin
                print week;
                for project:=1 step 1 until 8 do
                print a[project,week];
                print weekcost[week]
        end
end;
```

JOB PLANNING: A PROBLEM IN OPTIMIZATION   81

10.6 Results from the program

The program when run with the data quoted in 10.1 gave the following results.

Meancost   423·125

Project	ssdev	Starting week
2	2540687·5	5
2	2348287·5	4
2	2147287·5	2
2	1887287·5	2
.	.	.
.	.	.
.	.	.
8	600687·5	1
4	575087·5	18
4	567287·5	17
7	550287·5	14
7	524287·5	13

Week No.	\multicolumn{8}{c}{PROJECT}	Weekcost Total
	1	2	3	4	5	6	7	8	
1	50	80	0	0	0	0	0	50	180
2	50	80	0	0	0	0	0	60	
3	50	80	0	0	0	0	0	70	200
4	100	80	0	0	0	0	0	80	260
5	100	80	0	0	0	0	0	90	270
6	180	150	0	0	0	0	0	100	350
7	150	150	0	0	0	0	0	200	500
8	150	150	0	0	0	0	0	200	500
9	280	150	0	0	0	0	0	90	440
10	200	150	0	0	0	0	0	80	430
11	100	200	0	0	0	0	0	70	370
12	100	200	0	0	0	0	0	0	300
13	100	200	40	0	0	0	100	0	440
14	100	300	40	0	0	0	100	0	340
15	0	300	50	0	0	0	200	0	550
16	0	300	50	0	0	0	200	0	550
17	0	100	60	90	0	0	150	0	400
18	0	100	60	90	0	0	350	0	600
19	0	100	70	90	0	0	350	0	610
.									
.									
31	0	0	50	0	100	180	0	0	330
32	0	0	50	0	50	80	0	0	180

10.7 Comments on the program and results

Whilst the results from most computers are obtained in numerical form only, some provide facilities for presenting graphs. In some problems the results are more meaningful when presented in this way, and where these facilities are available there are usually Algol procedures available to enable the additional equipment to be used.

This problem would benefit from such a type of output. Figure 10/4 gives the graph of the original starting values and the final values. For completeness, Figure 10/3 gives the final arrangement of starting times for projects, so that it may be compared with that of Figure 10/1.

Using an Elliott 803, the time of computation on this particular problem was just short of 30 minutes. This represents a realistic amount of time for a problem which is never going to yield a perfect result. Other criteria for the best possible arrangement can easily be substituted into the program.

One suggestion might be to replace the squaring of the deviations by the positive value of the deviations. This would have the advantage of reducing the time taken in the execution of the program, and might give almost as good an answer.

As well as making variations to the program, it is also possible to consider whether there are better starting arrangements for the data.

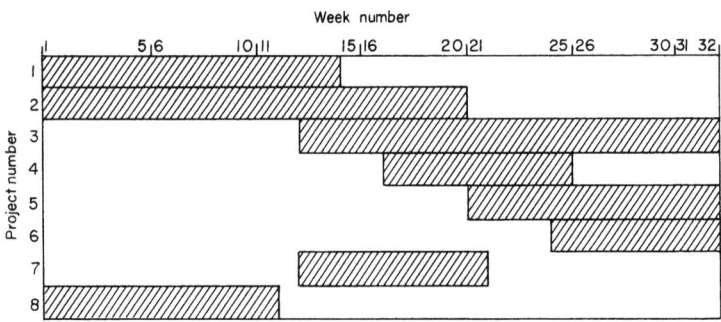

Figure 10/3 - Final Arrangement of Projects

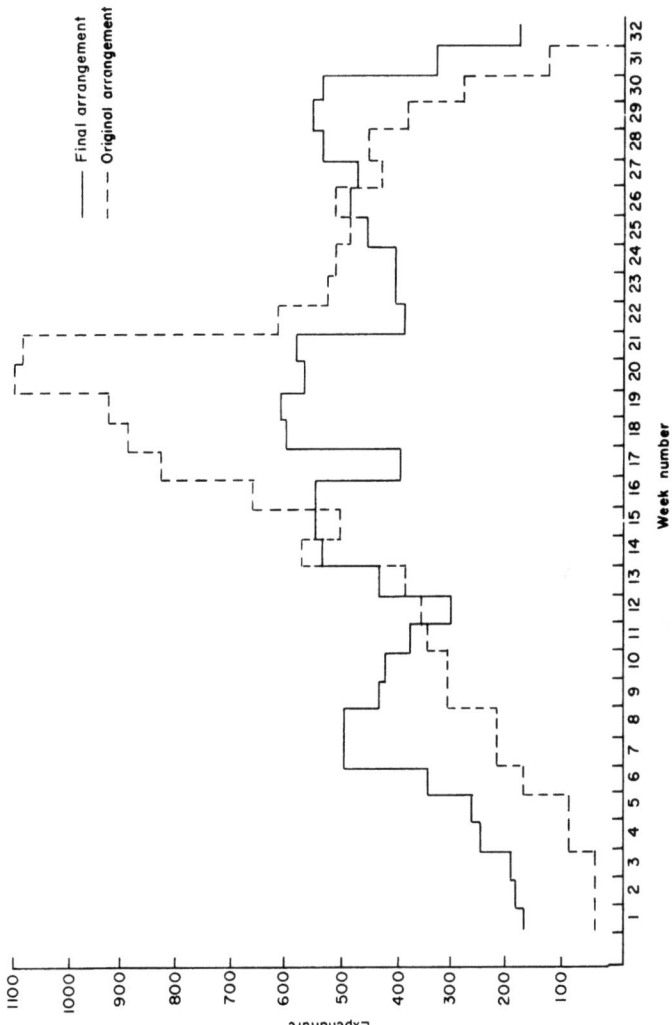

11

EVALUATION OF e

11.1 The problem

The number e is one of the fundamental constants of mathematics.
  Its value is given by the sum of the infinite series:
$$1 + \frac{1}{1!} + \frac{1}{2!} + \frac{1}{3!} + \ldots$$
  Using this series, it is required to calculate the value of e accurate to a specified number of decimal places.

11.2 The method and its application

A. The initial approach to this problem would appear to be straightforward.
  Successive terms of the series may be calculated from the previous term using a <u>for</u> statement, each term being compared with a constant $10^{-(n+1)}$ where n is the number of decimal places required.
  Thus the core of the program would be

<u>for</u> $m:=m+1$ <u>while</u> $term \geqslant 10\uparrow(-n-1)$ <u>do</u>
<u>begin</u>
    $term:=term/m;$
    $e:=e+term$
<u>end</u>;

  Detailed consideration of this approach reveals, however, that a satisfactory value of e will only be obtained for values of n which are less than the number of significant decimal digits which the computer can store for any given real variable. Thus for most of the modern computers a satisfactory solution would be yielded by the above algorithm for a value of n up to 7.
  B. To obtain a more general solution for, say, up to

EVALUATION OF e

1000 decimal places an alternative approach is needed.
   An acceptable method is to consider each required
digit of the solution to be a separate integer variable.
   We, therefore, consider two Algol integer arrays:
$$term\ [0:n+4] \quad \text{and} \quad e\ [0:n+4]$$
where the elements of the first array are to contain
the digits of the term currently being processed and
the second array is to hold the ultimate digits of
the solution.
   For accuracy up to 1000 decimal places, 4 extra
places must be calculated on each term to prevent
rounding error affecting the last place of the solution. Elementary analysis shows that the value of e
is less than 10. So we can safely assume that $e[0]$
will hold the integer part of e leaving $e[1:n]$ for
the fractional part.
   The core of the Algol program, embodying the calculation of successive terms of the series will then
be

```
    for m:=m+1 while sum≠0 do
    begin
        sum:=0;
        for i:=0 step 1 until n+4 do
        if term [i]≠0 then
        begin
            int:=term [i] ÷m;
            if i≠n+4 then
            term [i+1] :=term [i+1]
            +10×(term [i] -m×int);
            term [i] :=int;
            e [i] :=e [i] +int
        end
    end;
```

The above for-loop can, of course, make an element of the array e greater than 9, and some elements
could reach a 4-digit integer for values of n up to
1000. Another loop is thus necessary to split these
4-digit integers into 4 single digits which are added
into the appropriate elements of the final array. By
performing this process starting at the least significant end of the array and working upwards a single
digit will remain in each element of the array e.

11.3 The accuracy of the calculation

Since all arithmetic is carried out in integer

mode, the accuracy of the solution is guaranteed.

It should be noted in the full program of 11.4 that rounding has been performed on the nth decimal place.

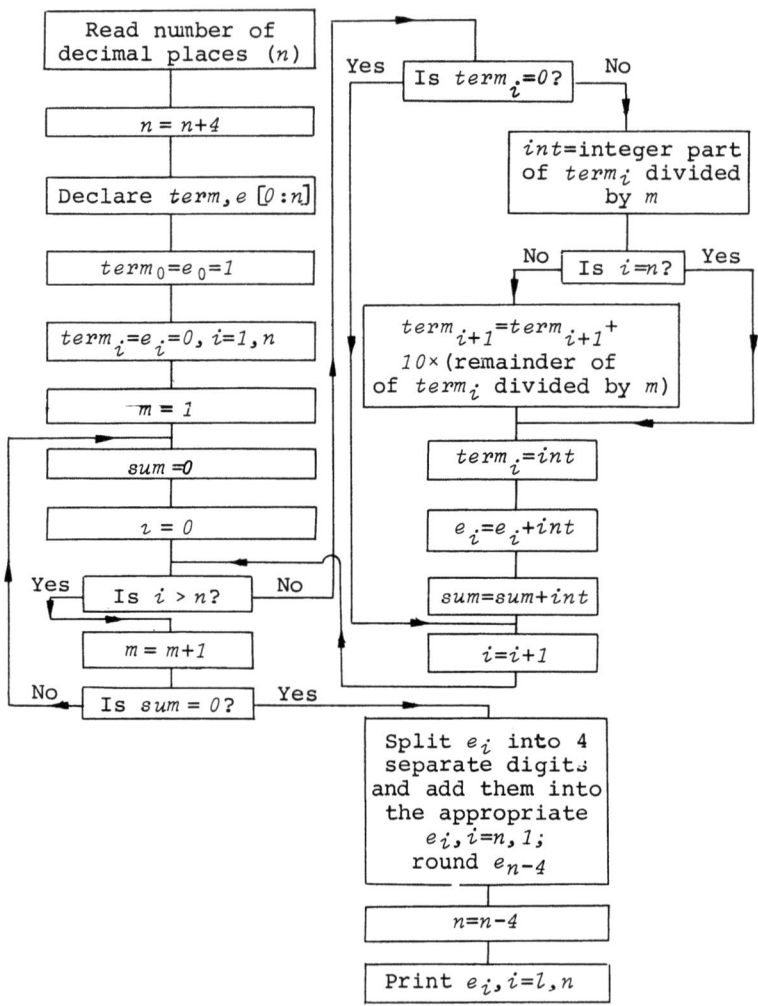

Figure 11/1 - Flow diagram for evaluation of e

11.4 The program

A flow diagram is given in Figure 11/1.

Evaluation of e;
<u>begin</u>
    <u>integer</u> *n;*
    <u>read</u> *n;*
    n:=n+4;
    <u>begin</u>
        <u>integer</u> *i,j,m,int,sum;*
        <u>integer</u> <u>array</u> *term,e [0:n];*
        term [0] :=e [0] :=1;
        <u>for</u> *i:=1* <u>step</u> *1* <u>until</u> *n* <u>do</u> *term [i] :=e [i] :=0;*
        <u>for</u> *m:=1,m+1* <u>while</u> *sum≠0* <u>then</u>
        <u>begin</u>
            sum:=0;
            <u>for</u> *i:=0* <u>step</u> *1* <u>until</u> *n* <u>do</u>
            <u>if</u> *term [i]≠0* <u>then</u>
            <u>begin</u>
                int:=term [i] ÷m;
                <u>if</u> *i≠n* <u>then</u>
                term [i+1] :=term [i+1]
                +10×(term [i] -m×int);
                term [i] :=int;
                e [i] :=e [i]+int;
                sum:=sum+int
            <u>end</u>
        <u>end</u>;
        <u>for</u> *i:=n* <u>step</u> *-1* <u>until</u> *1* <u>do</u>
        <u>begin</u>
            <u>if</u> *i=n-4* <u>then</u>
            e [i] :=e [i]+e [i+1] ÷5;
            <u>comment</u> *rounding;*
            <u>for</u> *j:=3,2,1* <u>do</u>
            <u>if</u> *i≥j* <u>then</u>
            <u>begin</u>
                sum:=10↑j;
                int:=e [i] ÷sum;
                e [i-j] :=e [i-j]+int;
                e [i] :=e [i] -sum×int
            <u>end</u>
        <u>end</u>;
        n:=n-4;
        <u>for</u> *i:=0* <u>step</u> *1* <u>until</u> *n* <u>do</u> <u>print</u> *e [i]*
    <u>end</u>
<u>end</u>;

88   PROGRAMMING BY CASE STUDIES

11.5 The results

Since two methods are discussed, results of the evaluation of *e* for both are shown below.

It can be seen that the first method (A) deviates from a true solution after 8 decimal places which is due to the accuracy with which the computer used can hold a real variable.

No. of decimal places required	Method (A)	Method (B) by program in 11.4
5	2·71828	2·71828
6	2·71828 2	2·71828 2
7	2·71828 18	2·71828 18
8	2·71828 183	2·71828 183
9	2·71828 1834	2·71828 1828
10	2·71828 18343	2·71828 18285
11	2·71828 183435	2·71828 18284 6
15		2·71828 18284 59045
25		2·71828 18284 59045 23536 02875
50		2·71828 18284 59045 23536 02874 71352 66249 77572 47093 69996
100		2·71828 18284 59045 23536 02874 71352 66249 77572 47093 69995 95749 66967 62772 40766 30353 54759 45713 82178 52516 64274

11.6 Timing of program

From consideration of the method employed it is clear that the time taken to run the program of 11.4 on a computer is proportional to the number of decimal places required provided that this number is sufficiently large and, otherwise, it is more dependent on the number of terms in the series which are included in the computation.

The graph of Figure 11/2 shows the relative times for up to 100 places.

It is possible to effect a slight economy in running time by modifying the *for* statement in the program which calculates the digits of the next term in the series for *e* from the previous term.

By starting the division procedure at the first non-zero digit rather than at the most significant digit, the number of times which the counter i is increased is greatly reduced.

EVALUATION OF e

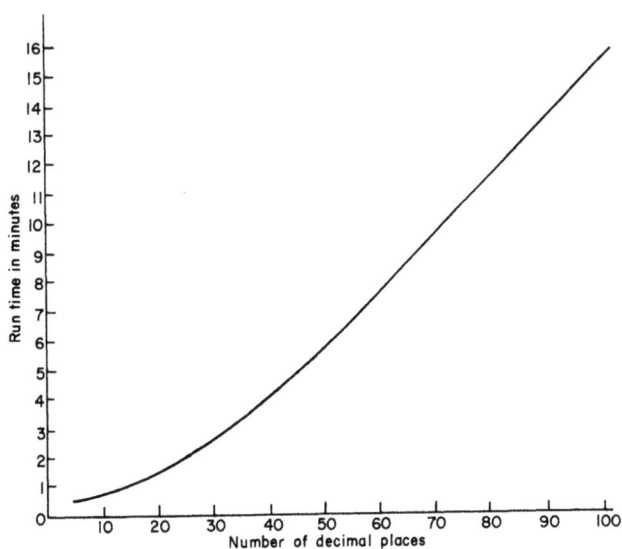

Figure 11/2 - Evaluation of e program run times

The additional programming consists of declaring and initially zeroising an integer variable, say, $istart$, and then the modified <u>for</u> statement becomes:

<u>for</u> $i:=istart$ <u>step</u> 1 <u>until</u> n <u>do</u>
<u>if</u> $term[i] \neq 0$ <u>then</u>
<u>begin</u>
    <u>if</u> $sum=0$ <u>then</u> $istart:=i;$
    $int:=term[i] \div m;$
    .
    .
    .
    $sum:=sum+int$
<u>end</u>;

The time saved by using the improved version of the program is of the order of half a minute over the straight line part of the graph in Figure 11/2.

INDEX

	Page		Page
abs	<u>7</u>,64	Function, standard	<u>7</u>
Actual parameter	<u>49</u>,64	Function designator	<u>50</u>,54,64
arctan	<u>7</u>,64	goto	<u>9</u>,18,24,28
Arithmetic expression	<u>6</u>	Identifier	<u>5</u>
Arithmetic operator	<u>6</u>	if	<u>10</u>,16,24,28
array	<u>13</u>,<u>47</u>,<u>50</u>	Input	<u>8</u>
Array	<u>13</u> <u>47</u>,14,16, <u>43</u>,<u>58</u>,75,79, 85	integer	<u>5</u>
		Label	<u>9</u>,18,24
Assignment statement	<u>7</u>,24,87	ln	<u>7</u>
		Name, call by	<u>50</u>
Basic symbol	<u>9</u>	Number	<u>5</u>
begin	<u>9</u>	Output	<u>8</u>
Block	<u>47</u>,87	Parameter	<u>49</u>,64
Bound	<u>47</u>,87	print	<u>9</u>
Bracket	<u>6</u>,<u>7</u>	Procedure	<u>49</u>,54,75,79
Call, procedure	<u>49</u>,<u>50</u>,58,80	Program	<u>9</u>
comment	<u>52</u>,64,87	read	<u>8</u>
Compound statement	<u>12</u>	real	<u>5</u>
Conditional statement	<u>10</u>,16,24,28	Relationship	<u>10</u>
Constant	<u>5</u>	sign	<u>7</u>,24
Controlled variable	<u>12</u>	sqrt	<u>7</u>,35,64
Declaration	<u>6</u>,<u>9</u>,<u>10</u>,<u>47</u>	step	<u>11</u>,16,35,38,<u>43</u>
do	<u>11</u>	subscript	<u>13</u>
Dummy statement	<u>12</u>,64	switch	<u>10</u>,18,24
else	<u>10</u>,64	then	<u>10</u>
end	<u>9</u>,<u>12</u>,64	Type	<u>5</u>
entier	<u>7</u>	until	<u>11</u>,16,35,38,<u>43</u>
Exponentiation	<u>6</u>,38		
for	<u>11</u>	value	<u>50</u>,54,64
For list element	<u>12</u>,<u>48</u>,87	Value, call by	<u>50</u>
For statement	<u>11</u>,<u>48</u>,16,35,<u>38</u>	Variable	<u>5</u>,13
Formal parameter	<u>49</u>,64	while	<u>48</u>,62,64,84,<u>85</u>

MIX
Papier aus verantwortungsvollen Quellen
Paper from responsible sources
FSC® C105338

If you have any concerns about our products,
you can contact us on
ProductSafety@springernature.com

In case Publisher is established outside the EU,
the EU authorized representative is:
Springer Nature Customer Service Center GmbH
Europaplatz 3, 69115 Heidelberg, Germany

Printed by Libri Plureos GmbH
in Hamburg, Germany